JOHN CLEESE

AND NOW FOR SOMETHING COMPLETELY DIFFERENT

John Cleese

AND NOW FOR SOMETHING COMPLETELY
DIFFERENT

Robert Gore Langton

André Deutsch Ltd is a subsidiary of **VCI plc**

www.vci.co.uk

CHAMELEON

First published in Great Britain in1999 by
Chameleon Books
an imprint of André Deutsch Ltd
76 Dean Street
London W1V 5HA

Copyright © **Essential Books 1999**

Design: **Neal Townsend** for **Essential**
Picture research: **Odile Schmitz** for **Essential**

The right of Robert Gore Langton to be
identified as the author of this work has been
asserted by him in accordance with the
Copyright, Designs and Patents act 1988

1 3 5 7 9 10 8 6 4 2

Reprographics by Jade Reprgraphics

Printed in Italy by Officine Grafiche DeAgostini

A catalogue record for this book is available
from the British Library

ISBN 0 233 99493 9

For Hal

ACKNOWLEDGEMENTS

The lion's share of thanks have to go to poor Sue for suffering in silence and shooing them away; to Georgia, Louis and Kit for the writing tips; my parents for letting me stay up; Jana Manova; Mal Peachey for the idea and patience; Jeremy Novick for the example; Anna for laughing; Jamie Muir for sympathy; Andrew Rissik for being a connoisseur; Michael and Rebecca; Geoffrey James; Tommy Steele; and the fine folks at the Westminster Reference Library.

INTRODUCTION

If you can remember watching the dot on the telly disappearing then you've hit middle-age. I can, I'm afraid, remember the dot, but I can't remember exactly when my brother and I cottoned onto John Cleese. Halfway through the first series of *Monty Python's Flying Circus*, I reckon. To my parents' infinite credit we were allowed to stay up late and watch, even in term time. Pyjamas and *Python* — a fabulous combination. It added to the pleasure that my father thought the programme was tripe.

Episodes of that series were prone to last-minute cancellation. One week we tuned in a couple of minutes late only to see some high seas adventure film starting. The disappointment at the loss of the week's entire laughter ration was crushing. Then as the tedious film's credits rolled, out there in the surf we spotted a desk. A desk with a man behind it, a BBC man who announced in bland tones of faultless continuity, 'And now for something completely different…'.

It was Cleese, of course, and I have never been so relieved to see anyone on TV in all my life. True, John wasn't the nicest or the cosiest. That was always Michael Palin. But he was tall and gaunt and funny; funny in a profound, physical way that you ascribe to only a handful of great comedians. Of course we all love Tommy and Eric and Ernie and Les and Frankie. But those frilly shirted Northern comics have all long since passed through the irony tunnel of the Nineties; their dated, slightly awful quality only adds to the affection you feel for them. But they belong to a vanished era — and so, maybe, do Cleese and co.

But thanks to Cleese and co. you could look at a congealed school dinner and say "where's the pleasure in that?" and get a laugh the length of the table. Non-fans hadn't a clue what you were on about.

When Cleese invented Torquay hotelier Basil Fawlty, well it was more joy. Twenty-five years on and my own daughter, who loves the series on video, issues orders suffixed with a curt "thank you so much", as if her parents were irksome guests in her hotel. Her brothers — used to being bossed — identify more with Manuel.

Cleese — where is the man behind the mayhem? Well, of course, like all funny men he's an enigma wrapped inside a conundrum, to half remember the saying. He'll hate this book. He had nothing to do with it. He'll mutter something about how Spike Milligan was funnier than he was. How *Python* was really pretty awful. How Basil ruined his life. He'll deny everything. He'll suggest I have therapy, or write my own sketches. May be he'll jump up and down like Basil yelling, 'What *is* the point?'

For those who want a detailed life, I recommend a very entertaining biography, *Cleese Encounters* (Orion) by Jonathan Margolis. For those who want the broadcasting pedantry — well, the Internet is heaving with web sites loaded with minutiae. This is a celebration of a career, not a dissection of a private life. But you do get some smashing pictures and a text that's written with gratitude.

COASTING

In fact, the rumour isn't quite true: John Cleese didn't change his name from Cheese. It was his father who did. Reginald Marwood Cheese decided to become Reginald Marwood Cleese on joining the army in 1915. He could face the bullets, apparently, but not the jokes about his name. Reg decided to insert the letter 'L' into his name after considering an 'R' — Creese — which is how the Japanese fans now address his famous son, John, anyway. His only son, John Marwood Cleese, was born in the West Country resort of Weston-super-Mare a few weeks after war broke out, on 27 October 1939. He is the only world-class comic to have emerged from that sleepy resort.

Considering how class-conscious a lot of John's later humour was, it's no surprise that his father entertained mild delusions of grandeur, having spent some time working in the East for the Union of Canton insurance company. Reg described himself on forms as a 'marine underwriter'. But while John was growing up, his father's daily routine wasn't based in some exotic far-flung colonial office. It consisted mostly of driving around Somerset in his Austin A10 to sell insurance.

The wild card in the family was John's grandfather, John Edwin Cheese. He was a

Right: Cleese as Mr Teabags, the minister of Silly Walks, on his way to the office. Cleese came to hate the walk and refused to do it after a while. A shame, as he has spiffing legs.

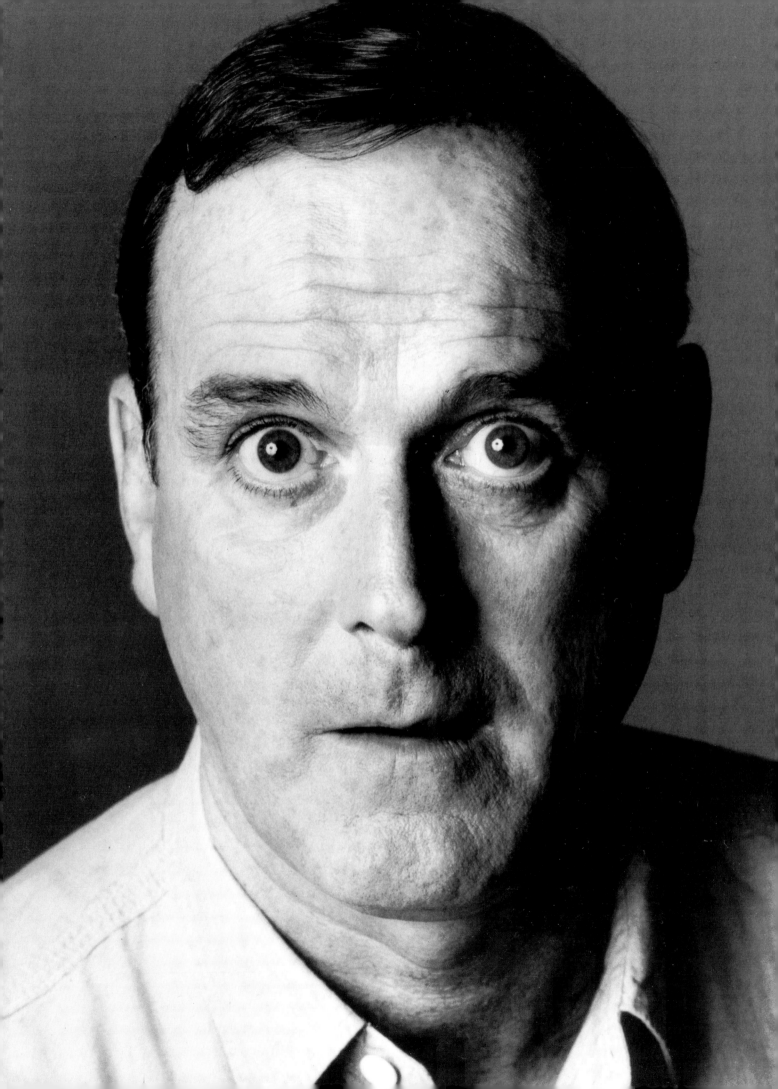

very crafty solicitor's clerk who — in a surreal touch — owned the entire office block in which he worked. No-one quite knew why, nor how much loot he had stashed away over the years, but there was a family story that had he put his money into railways he could have made a fortune. Anyway, he didn't and John's father had to make do with his £30-a-week salary. It was a 'decent screw', as they used to say, but there was no fat.

Muriel Cross, John's devoted mother, was the daughter of a local Weston worthy burger. She and Reg fell in love and did all the things that courting couples did in those days except that they did them comparatively late in life. Both parents, unusually for that time, were in their forties when their son and heir was born.

John may have had a rather remote relationship with his father, who was — by John's estimation — a very nice man. An only child, John was certainly not neglected. His mother coddled him too much, perhaps. Coddling would emerge in later life in several sketches written by and starring John, most famously in a *Monty Python* sketch featuring two old bags (Eric Idle and Terry Jones) itchy-cooing over the grown-up John as if he were still in his pram. 'Does he want his rattle?' they shrill; 'Can he talk?' they coo. 'Yes, of course I can talk. I am Minister for Overseas Development.' Much of that must have come from dear Muriel.

Certainly, the changing of the family name from Cheese to Cleese was far-sighted. This minor alteration of his name certainly spared young John a lot of torment as a child, especially as his friend at prep school would turn out to be a chap called Butter. Only Chalk would have been worse.

In later years when John came to perform the 'Cheese Shop' sketch again in *Python* (a customer goes into a cheese shop and proceeds to itemize dozens of different cheeses, each of which is 'fresh out'), Cleese delivered the litany of *fromages* with a genuine relish, suggesting some almost personal connection with the stuff. It is possible that somewhere along the line his ancestors had perhaps been cheese vendors. 'Blessed are the cheese-makers', as Christ is memorably misquoted in the Monty Python film *The Life of Brian*. John must have written that line. Whatever, for John, cheese has remained a tasty comestible, never a source of grief.

Left: Cleese, whose family name was Cheese, but was changed to Cleese shortly before the Somme offensive.

WESTON YEARS

The world of Weston-super-Mare, known locally as 'Weston-super-Mud', is a small town (the population in the year John left home was 40,361) which is twenty-one miles by road from Bristol, pointing out to sea towards Wales. It is the sort of place that — in its dreams — wants to be Bournemouth, and it is perhaps a key to Cleese the comic. Why? Because there are few places quite so English.

On a *South Bank Show* devoted to his life, John commented that the place was 'archetypally British lower-middle class. It had this strong puritan work ethic. People found it very hard to enjoy themselves. There was a pressure to conform, to be respectable and not to shock. You seldom saw people in Weston kissing each other; they patted or pecked each other. It was a place of repression really.' And the place rubbed off on him too.

Nearby Bristol, however, had glamour, despite the pasting Goering gave it. The city has always had a vivid thespian streak, and contains two nationally famous theatres in the Hippodrome and the Old Vic, the latter the oldest surviving rep in Britain. Bristol was once a training ground for talent, producing several stars including Archie Leach (alias Cary Grant) — a name Cleese would borrow for his own character in the film, *A Fish Called Wanda*.

Weston, on the other hand, has few other great names on its roll of honour, though Deborah Kerr and Jill Dando hailed from there too. It's hard to believe, but John claimed that when he and his parents moved out of their flat in Weston (they moved umpteen times to different rented properties), Jeffrey Archer and his parents moved in. Who knows, the two boys may even have shaken hands on the threshold. Imagine them in their shorts. Both destined for celebrity — one as a national figure of fun, the other the subject of this book.

Reg and Muriel were devoted parents, and made crippling financial sacrifices to give John a private education. At first he attended St Peter's Prep School in Weston (where he took the title role in *Scenes from Twelfth Night — the Tricking of Malvolio*), then as a dayboy at Clifton College in Bristol, a middle-drawer public school, where John, at 6'4" tall already, dwarfed all the masters.

Cleese in 'My brain hurts' mode.

It's the Arts! A fabulous sketch in which Cleese terminates an interview with a famous film director (Graham Chapman) with a bored "Oh shuddup". The Pythons sabotaged the earnest arty TV interview. Not that it put Melvyn Bragg off.

If you are going to be a comedian, public school is a good place to start. Certainly, the public schools were churning out the talent of the day. Shrewsbury alone had produced William Rushton, Richard Ingrams and Michael Palin. But Clifton hadn't yet come up with anyone who was funny. Not unless you include Sir Henry Newbolt, who wrote the famous poem 'Vita Lampada' about manliness and trying hard at games. Each stanza ends with 'Play up! play up! and play the game!'

The poem expressed precisely the sort of faintly homosexual, team-inspired public school madness (very *Monty Python*) that made young men rub Bovril on each other's chests before matches and led Britain, tragically, to treat World War I as an away match. John found school, with its compulsory sense of team spirit and air of uneventful tediousness, completely lacking in any sort of intellectual challenge.

The only other distinguished Cliftonian in history was Field Marshal Haig, the great widow maker of the 1914–18 debacle. Haig was a dismally unimaginative man (though he would be revered by Basil Fawlty, as a man with real sex appeal). His style of leadership was pilloried mercilessly in *Oh What a Lovely War*, a theatrical landmark in the 1960s satire boom, in which Cleese was to play a significant part.

Without any native Cliftonian entertainers to nurture him, Cleese amused himself by developing the subtle art of classroom subversion, though never so obviously that he was rusticated, birched or (to borrow an example from Michael Palin's TV spoof, *Tomkinson's Schooldays*) fed to the school leopard. He had a talent for sums too, winning a mathematics scholarship which was worth £36 a year to his parents. However, old boys now recall Cleese as being a bit... well, bland at school. Funny, but bland. It's curious how people frequently say the same things about the early lives of comics as they do about serial killers who lived next door — 'bland', 'a bit of a loner', 'nice to his mum', and so forth.

At the time, young Cleese was actually busy watering the pot plant that would blossom into a career. He never missed an episode of *The Goon Show*, and took to writing down snippets of the material to enliven dull lessons. And he was always scribbling down items from American sitcoms of the 1950s in his school diary. A keen sportsman, John eventually made the first eleven in cricket and he once succeeded in removing the great Dennis Compton (caught Whitty, bowled Cleese) when Clifton played the MCC. The incident would reappear in a future Fawlty-ism: 'Well, whose fault is it, you cloth-eared bint? Dennis Compton's?' The character of Basil, John's alter ego, occasionally drew on the Cleese biography.

Cleese has always maintained he was a meek boy, feeble and much bullied. On the *South Bank Show* he confessed: 'People don't believe it but I have a meek streak. I remember my father coming down to watch me play in a football match and finding three people sitting on top of me. I had a lot of problems asserting normal healthy aggression.' Something he later made sure Basil Fawlty never suffered from.

The world in which Cleese grew up was a drab one by today's standards, but it was a quiet one: the country longed for some uneventfulness after the war years. At the time the food was dreadful, wine was for the few and rock'n'roll was yet to be born. Variety was in its death throes and television, which had yet to find a mass audience, was not important. (And the TV sets took *forever* to warm up.) West End theatres were still full of plays with French windows and well-spoken casts. British films were, well, mostly cosy. The Cold War was a non-event on an island which was only just putting on weight after years of rationing. New comedy, such as it was, remained confined to the wireless.

ACCOUNTANCY? NO, THANKS

John was bullied at school and, like so many before and since, resorted to comedy as the best form of defence. He appeared as Lucifer in a school production of Marlowe's *Dr Faustus* and got huge laughs merely by walking on stage. The other boys seemed to find John naturally entertaining, even when he wasn't trying to be. As a mimic, he soon got most of the masters off to a tee.

Eventually he emerged from his school with his three science A-levels. He had to find something to do — get a job, have a career complete with pension. 'The reason I think why accountancy used to feature so hugely in my sketches was the gentle pressure from my parents — who were very kind — to become an accountant,' he told Melvyn Bragg on the *South Bank Show* years later.

The comic attacks on accountancy started early. There's a sketch in the *1948 Show* (*Monty Python*'s immediate precursor) in which John, Marty Feldman, Tim Brooke-Taylor and Graham Chapman are all sitting around, explaining in turns: 'I'm a chartered accountant.' They all have their say, then it's John's turn. Poker-faced in suit and bowler hat, this accountant simply says '… and I am a gorilla.' That was in 1964.

Python mocked the profession so effectively that to admit to being a chartered accountant by the 1970s was brave. Indeed, a celebrated *Python*-inspired T-shirt slogan of the time read: 'Accountancy! More exciting than lion taming!' By rejecting accountancy, John was arguably also discarding the little world of Weston, that world he defined as being archetypally British. 'There was a pressure to conform and not to shock,' he said, again to Melvyn Bragg. 'Also, there was this very strong puritan work ethic: people found it very hard to enjoy themselves. I have always had a feeling my own feelings were being held in,' he claimed.

John wanted to go university to read Law, an ambition of his which had never been seriously entertained by his parents. However, the faithful Reg and Muriel (for whom university was a wildly posh concept) came to his aid, providing the cash for an extra Oxbridge term. John came up with the academic goods and duly won a place at Downing College, Cambridge.

No schoolboy of that era could get through school without a dose of square bashing in the school army corps. In the days of National Service, corps was the warm-up for full-time army life. The army and Cleese (who was officer material without really knowing it) were destined to rub along quite happily without each other. But the experience of life in uniform was to prove important: the army was to become another mainstay of his comedic career. If there was one rule in the British Army, it was the mantra of that *Python* Australian sketch: 'No pooftas!' John's response was to create sketches which suggested that the institution was littered with mad people and handbag-swinging gay boys.

It's now largely forgotten, but in one lovely *Python* sketch a recruiting officer debates fashion design in the British Army with a potential recruitee. 'Now, if you want a regiment of the line that's really saying something about interior decor, then you've *got* to go for the Durham Light Infantry.' What could be more subversive — or delightfully harmless — than the idea of the British Army taking a keen and sensitive interest in the world of interiors?

A senior army officer was a stock character throughout the *Python* years. Always played by Graham Chapman, with a swagger stick, he would frequently appear and put a stop to sketches that had become too silly. If *Python* was going to mock authority, it made some kind of perverse sense to have an officer interrupting the show and telling it to pull its socks up.

By the time Cleese arrived at Cambridge he knew nothing about girls. Even later he was still, like most single-sex educated boys, totally inexperienced. He did, however, have one unrequited affair. He fell in love with a local bright-eyed and bushy-tailed young thing — a ring-tailed lemur.

'I have adored lemurs ever since I first met a ring-tailed lemur at Bristol Zoo in 1954', he would publicly confess three decades later in a fine television documentary devoted to these cuddly Madagascan tree-dwellers. Curiously enough, the faces of the lemurs — middle-aged, aldermanic-looking creatures — bore a striking resemblance to the sort of civic dignitaries you might expect to meet in Weston-super-Mare whose very blandness John found so endlessly fascinating.

Poor old Weston! It had, after all, done him no harm. But John himself remained

---

Overleaf: Did you know the whale is an insect? The Secret Policeman's Ball: Cleese performs the "interesting facts" sketch with Peter Cook, the comedy guru for successive generations of comics.

ambivalent about the place. It had proved a kindly and supportive place of refuge in which to grow up, but he returned to it time and time again for comedy material. In the *Python* sketches, Weston comes up time and again as a world of brown linoleum parlours, respectability, snobbishness and a deep-seated fear of social embarrassment. Cleese saw it as a world of shopkeepers, accountants, Rotarians, hoteliers and a legion of 'Mrs Niggerbaiters', the old crones in *Monty Python* who squawked like the old women who wandered Weston's draughty streets. To Cleese, the Englishness of Weston was both friend and foe. He cunningly staked it out as his comic territory.

'MR CLEESE, SIR.' THE PREP SCHOOL MASTER

'Had he not become famous I would certainly still remember him as a nice, pleasant young master who told us about how to play practical jokes,' recalls Geoffrey James, a TV producer and former pupil of the young teacher, John Cleese, in 1958. 'Except for the fact that he was prone to endless digressions and red herrings.'

John had two years to kill before he could go to Downing College, Cambridge, since there were so many students waiting to take up deferred places, thanks to National Service. Instead of travelling the world and doing the things that students now routinely do, he grew a beard and went back to his old prep school, St Peter's, to teach geography, history and games. The naughty iconoclastic boy at Clifton had turned — briefly — into the athletic master to whom all the pupils looked up.

'He had a beard, he was enthusiastic, funny and I remember he gave us sweets,' remembers James. 'No-one else did that. He taught me geography. He was funny because of all the diversions in class — he told us stories about practical joking. How, when he was at Clifton during rag week, they went along to a group of workmen and warned them that a group of students disguised as policeman were going to tell them not to dig up the road. Then they went to the police and told them students impersonating workmen were illegally digging up the road... you know, standard student pranks.

'John also told us with some pride about a secret expedition down to the nearby

Left: Cleese with sideburns in his young comic days, when the BBC were up his trousers.

traders' market, where the stallholders put up their canvas awnings with poles stuck into special holes in the ground. John and his class went down there and filled up the holes with concrete. Fantastically irritating for the stallholders, but we enjoyed the story.

'John was very keen on sport, too. He was fanatical about football — which he coached — and he did a lot to encourage me. He even persuaded my father to buy me some very expensive football boots — six guineas they were, a fortune at the time. He was very sporty and a serious non-smoker — he abhorred it. I was amazed to see him years later on TV doing an interview with a fag in his hand.

'Was he any good as a teacher of geography? Probably not, but he got our attention. We had a lot of fun. I was summoned to see him in the master's common room once. He was filling in *The Times* crossword with utter loathing, just writing in any old letters at high speed. I said, "Sir, why are you doing that — it doesn't make any sense." He said, "No, it doesn't make any sense to you and me, boy, but it makes a lot of sense to the other masters who think I'm brilliant." '

Incidentally, among his other schoolmasterly duties, John manned the projector for the school films which were shown on wet afternoons. One of those movies was *The Lavender Hill Mob*, the Ealing comedy starring Alec Guinness as the snaggle-toothed master criminal. The director was Michael Crichton who would, thirty years later, also direct John's masterpiece, *A Fish Called Wanda...*

FUN IN THE FENS

Students first turned up at Cambridge in 1209, no doubt parking their donkeys illegally, being sick in the canals and bouncing cheques in the local taverns. By 1960 Cambridge was still a great place to be a student. True, sexual intercourse hadn't officially begun, the Cold War hadn't yet thawed into the Summer of Love and Cambridge was full of so many petty rules that it must have seemed like a kindergarten for very large infants. But the nation's youthful performing elite, John included, was gearing itself up for a mass attack of cheekiness. The so-called satire

Right: Cleese with David Niven in the truly abysmal 1970 film The Statue. *The plot revolved around a 20-ft statue of Niven with an enormous male organ.*

boom was cooking and Cambridge University was its wok.

Oxford is the city of dreaming spires; Cambridge, according to the old joke, is the city of perspiring dreams. Whereas Oxford was woolly, romantic and socially smarter, Cambridge was the home of swots and clear-eyed logic. Graeme Garden, the boffin in *The Goodies* TV show, was a classic example of the Cambridge species. John, with his flair for logical analysis, was likewise perfectly suited to it.

At Clifton John had been socially inferior because he was a day-boy. Now he was a public schoolboy among a largely grammar school comedy crowd. With a cool efficiency, he had worked out what the examiners required in his A-levels and he had done well. A law degree should be a doddle. At school he was shy, a loner and, in retrospect, a bit of a star. Now he was at Cambridge, a small fish in a deep and crowded pond.

Almost the first thing Cleese did was to join The Footlights, the famous but rather ghastly all-male dinner jacket club (women were only admitted later under Eric Idle's presidency) that was essential for anyone with an eye to the stage. Footlights performers Peter Cook and Jonathan Miller, along with Dudley Moore and Alan Bennett (from Oxford) had already triumphed with their landmark show, *Beyond The Fringe*, which was a big commercial hit. There was much to play for.

For reasons no-one has explained, Cambridge proved amazingly fertile ground for comedy in the 1960s, producing *Private Eye* magazine, The Establishment Club (short-lived, but influential), several shows, plus the embryo of both *Monty Python's Flying Circus* and *The Goodies*.

At Cambridge a young David Frost was well on his way to becoming God. He would soon be employing ex-Cambridge writers in pioneering material on the new commercial station, ITV, where he made his name fronting *That Was The Week That Was*. When Cleese went up, Peter Cook was the big comedy cheese in Cambridge. Miles funnier than anyone else then on the comedy scene, he was already being imitated by younger undergraduates.

If you wanted to be funny at Cambridge, the competition was serious. You turned up in your cavalry twills, tweed jacket and woolly tie at the Societies Fair and there was young Frostie, in charge of the Footlights stall. Not yet with clipboard in hand, but looking pretty much like the benign, hood-eyed reptile he now resembles.

A fresh-faced Graham Chapman — then a medical student — duly rolled up. It

Cleese significantly posed at the centre of the Python *team.*
Would you let any of them into your home?

turned out that you couldn't just join The Footlights, you had to be invited. 'So what's the point of the stall?' asked Chapman. 'Er, there isn't one,' replied Frost. You had to be invited to join, and to be invited you had to audition. John had the same problem as Graham. Asked what he could do, John hazarded a guess: 'I suppose I try to make people laugh.' In time, the two got together in a coffee house and wrote sketches for various 'Smokers' (heats for the big annual revue). It was all very complicated and rule-bound.

Cleese and Chapman unwittingly formed a writing partnership that was to last

for years. Chapman, the pipe-smoking son of a Leicestershire policeman, was in training for serious alcoholism. He was also homosexual, though that was only just beginning to dawn on him. John was working hard, playing cricket and football for his college, and hanging around with Tim Brooke-Taylor, Bill Oddie and Chris Stuart-Clarke. Cleese and Graham promptly got down to the difficult business of sketch writing. A revue show — *Double Take* (1962) — to which John contributed several items, and in which he also performed alongside Chapman, would prove a winner. John's slightly embarrassing blurb in the programme read:

'Bluff, slate-faced, 22-year-old Registrar, he reads Law and plays soccer for Downing. He grew his beard to avoid being mistaken for Pete Murray: an enthusiast for verbal humour, he is nevertheless prepared to stoop to slapstick, where he rates the custard pie above the banana skin. He has a laugh which is coarse and ingenious to boot: he says he cannot sing and keeps a locked piano in his room to prove it.'

In the event *Double Take* became, after a spot of recasting (Chapman left to become a doctor in London), *A Clump Of Plinths* — a lovely title which was decided upon after the original *You Can't Call A Show 'Cornflakes'* was rejected. Tim Brooke-Taylor and Cleese remained in the cast, joined by Bill Oddie and Humphrey Barclay. The show's title was then changed to *Cambridge Circus*, which must have left bewildered punters wondering where the animals were. It was a hit, full of nonsense as usual, and John's antics were developing nicely. He was on his way.

SHOWBIZ & LOVE

By then John had fallen hopelessly in love, but whoever she was, she wasn't interested in him and history doesn't relate the outcome of the affair. However, there were immediate repercussions for the young Cleese. 'I couldn't cope at all. I couldn't get any work done,' John confessed in a *Daily Mail* interview years later. 'She didn't fall in love with me and she was well advised not to. If I'm soft now, I was a wimp then. No girl is interested in someone who just adores her.'

The actress Miriam Margolyes was at Cambridge at the same time as John and

Left: With the Norwegian blue parrot – perhaps the greatest comedy sketch ever written for TV. The plastic mac was a homage to Peter Cook.

she wasn't a *Python* fan: 'I was there with all the *Monty Python* people. I loathed them and they loathed me. They didn't think I was funny and they weren't interested in whether I was funny or not. You see, they're not actually interested in women. They play all the women's parts, and they play them in bold caricature.'

She has a point, but she excused John, saying, 'the only one who's allowed women any prominence is Cleese in *Fawlty Towers*.' The trouble was, John simply didn't know what to say to women: 'Some of us were almost inconceivably inexperienced so far as women were concerned. And there would have been very little point writing about women since they were from another planet as far as I was concerned.' Problems in his relationships with women would only really be ironed out after three marriages and years of therapy. John left Cambridge in 1963 and went off to tour the *Cambridge Circus* show in New Zealand; it was in Auckland that, in a fit of absent-mindedness, he finally lost his virginity.

Romance aside, by the mid-1960s The Footlights was basically a dry run for a showbiz career. Eric Idle wasn't far off the mark when he said, 'Certainly, in your last year you were nobody if you didn't have at least three agents coming to look at you in a Smoker.' John had his doubts about giving up the Law, but he pressed on with performing. By the time he finished and opted for a career in comedy, the three years of training at the taxpayers' expense had ultimately produced one ten-minute courtroom sketch. However, the pay-off for persisting with comedy was immediate.

The BBC were looking for new talent. In *The Life of Python* by George Perry, John remembers an early visit from their scouts: 'There were these two guys in grey suits. I suddenly realised that they were offering me a job at the BBC. I was supposed to be joining a firm of solicitors in the City called Freshfields at £12 a week and here they were offering £30. So I went with them.' *Cambridge Circus*, meanwhile, had been signed for a West End transfer: 'Suddenly we were young people who were successful and were having newspaper articles written about us,' John observed. Reg and Muriel's worries about his future career as a solicitor were thus allayed — the BBC money was good and, joy of joys, the job came with a pension plan.

In a way, theatre would have been a good choice for him, but John was a performer, not an actor; a sketch writer, not a playwright. And just as well. All plays at the BBC — including revues such as *Cambridge Circus* — had to be vetted by the Lord Chamberlain. When John was an aspiring comic, the holder of this dusty office was the eleventh Earl of Scarborough, a former governor of Bombay and author of the none too racy, *History Of The Eleventh Hussars*. Only in England, surely, could a man with military credentials be put in charge of overseeing scripts by the likes of John Osborne and Spike Milligan. It was a gloriously daft and very British state of affairs. No wonder Cleese found such rich pickings in the army and other national institutions.

Radio and TV were no more liberated than the army, but they were less hassle. Anyway, the comedy boom was well and truly on and John was now on the road to showbiz success. He was still very public school — cliquey and aloof — but his deadpan, barrister-like style already had a cult following in varsity circles. However, the comedy that he was writing was almost totally derivative: 'My early humour I just pinched from everyone else,' he admits. Chief mentor was Peter Cook, who had created his E L Wisty character while still at school.

'Cook's influence was so thick you could cut it with a knife... he can make a perfectly blunt and banal statement sound so funny, just by the choice of words,' John told Melvyn Bragg. 'When I started to write for BBC Radio I did a series of conversations at a bus stop for Derek Guyler and Dick Emery. They were all based on Peter Cook's "interesting facts" sketches — "Did you know the whale is an insect that feeds on bananas?", that sort of thing.'

John didn't go down that well with the critics in *Cambridge Circus*; they preferred Bill Oddie and Tim Brooke-Taylor. But he did get a mention for his gimlet eyes and his sketch-writing ability. 'Judge Not' — a skit about a midget in a witness box (that lawyer thing again) — was regarded as an instant classic, and the 1965 album of the show is now a collector's item.

In the meantime the BBC was giving John scripts to play with. He was now colluding with all the Light Entertainment crowd and was also submitting material to *That Was The Week That Was* and pilots for what was to become the hugely successful radio show, *I'm Sorry I'll Read That Again*. He took to writing for the radio rather well — it suited his talent for verbal contortionism. Four months after leaving

Overleaf: the sketch about flying sheep. Ovine aviation was a real possibility for depressed sheep. Why Cleese and Palin were dressed as French onion sellers is now unclear.

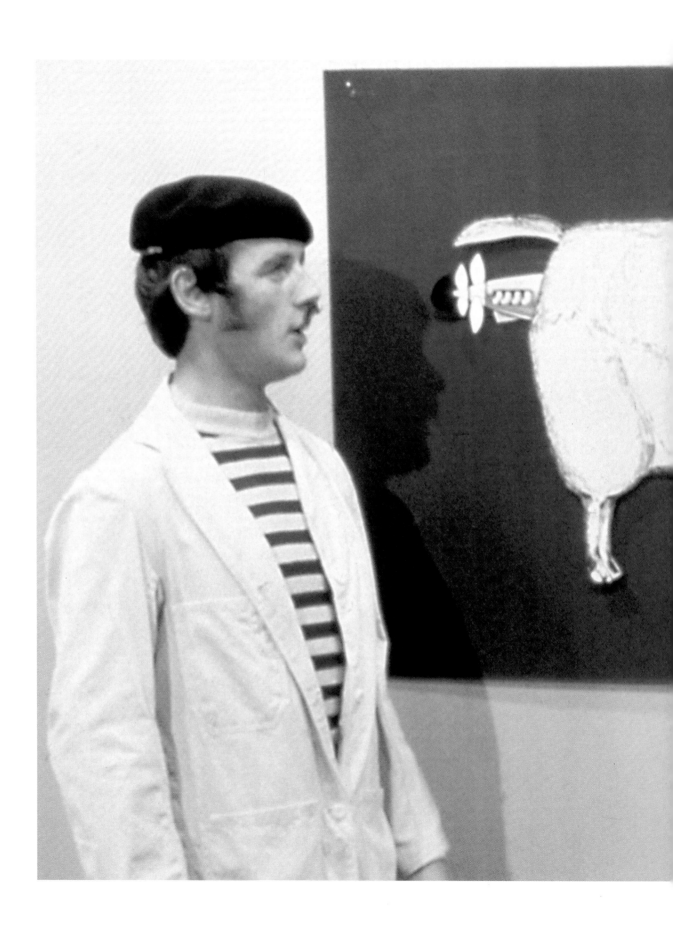

Cambridge, John was working on jokes for Terry Scott and Brian Rix in *Yule Be Surprised*, *The Dick Emery Show*, and *Not To Worry* with Ronnie Barker and Cyril Fletcher — not bad for a 24-year-old ex-academic.

CLEESE: MR MUSICAL

*C*ambridge Circus ended up in New York. The show ran smoothly and when it closed there was no reason to rush back home. Besides, while he was out there John found himself being asked to audition for a part in the Broadway production of *Half A Sixpence*. The show was based on H G Wells' novel *Mr Kipps* and Tommy Steele (who had liked Cleese in *Cambridge Circus*) was to play Arthur Kipps. After a disastrous audition in which he couldn't sing a note but was very funny, John secured the part of the English cad, Young Walsingham, who steals all Arthur's money.

It all went swimmingly until it went wrong, as musicals have a habit of doing. The director was fired and his replacement was Gene Saks, a kick-ass Broadway hardnut. Broadway directors all have terrible trouble in understanding the British sense of humour. The American public never let that worry them: vast numbers of Americans would come to enjoy *Monty Python* while completely missing a great deal of its peculiarly English humour. Anyway, *Half A Sixpence* opened in 1965 in Toronto and ended up being a hit on Broadway.

It was the old story: sweetness and light on stage, World War III backstage. John seemed to have enjoyed the whole experience, though. The idea of Tommy Steele and John performing in a musical is in itself rather glorious. Surely musical theatre and the lanky comic could never mix? The humorous song had been a fall-back in Footlights revues since time immemorial; John, however, went out of his way to stop people singing in sketches. Besides, in musicals you need to be able to smile a lot, and John was always incapable of looking convincing when happy.

Tommy Steele, on the other hand, can do nothing but look happy, his mouth permanently set in a grin of joy. He remembers John well: 'He didn't have a great part, though he seemed to enjoy the show. He was brilliant in it.' It would come as

The first Python feature film, Monty Python and The Holy Grail *(1975) was shot in damp conditions in Scotland. The imitation chainmail necessitated large quantities of recycled string pants.*

no surprise to old St Peter's pupils that backstage John was still up to his old crossword tricks. Tommy remains unaware of Cleese's literary duplicity to this day, judging from the following:

'He was a lovely fella. He used to come into rehearsals in the morning, make himself a cup of coffee and sit there doing *The Times* crossword. He must have got the paper from London, a week late maybe. Anyway he just sat there doing the clues. John to me was a complete mystery.' Why? 'I couldn't understand how he was so quick with those crosswords.'

WAITRESSING & ROMANCE

Still, never mind half a sixpence, John was by now earning $200 a week. At this point in his life, like Jimmy Cagney, he was 'top of the world, ma'. Not that his mother ever heard from him; Cleese rarely wrote home and Muriel must have well and truly laid into him about it when he eventually got back.

Around this time, Cleese had an aborted stab at journalism. However, after a six-week stint on *Newsweek* magazine, he decided to quit before he was fired. If anything, the brief career change does suggest that perhaps showbiz wasn't intellectual enough for the young Cleese and that he was having doubts about it; with Cleese life was, and remains, a series of doubts. With his vision of a career in the Law now on a rapidly receding horizon, John's cerebral streak had never really been satisfied, and becoming editor of the *New York Times* must have seemed appealing for a while.

Still, in matters of the heart things had definitely picked up. Cleese had met an exceptionally pretty young girl in a restaurant. Her name was Connie Booth and she was a waitress. After paying the bill, John invited her out — there is surely no more effective way of chatting a girl up than offering her free tickets to come and watch you in a hit play. Needless to say, Connie was in analysis at the time (New York was full of it, even then), something that was to play a significant part in both their lives. Of course, in the years to come she would return to waitressing; as Polly, she helped Manuel with the dishes at that fine Torquay establishment, Fawlty Towers.

By this time, John had also encountered Terry Gilliam, an odd young man from Medicine Lake, Minnesota. Gilliam was to become the *Pythons'* resident cartoonist and, of course, a brilliantly imaginative film-maker. His animations were central to the series and he introduced one of the most enduring images of *Monty Python* (the six-toed cartoon foot borrowed from a painting by the Renaissance master, Bronzino), which came down with a fat raspberry sound, cutting off the show's oompah-ing signature tune. Gilliam was the only Yank in the team and he and the ultra-English Mr Cleese hit it off instantly.

Connie remained on the other side of the Atlantic and their affair became a long-distance arrangement. John came home, aged 26, still 6' 4 3/4" tall, wearing long

In Geneva Kon Rapp,
Kung-Fu fanatic
and cat-lover,
frivolously shoots
Mafia leader Enrico Marx,
a lively belly-dancer
at a Belgian disco . . .

Eric Idle was always cheerful about being killed. Cleese's maniacal Lancelot turns The Holy Grail *into a blood bath. The publicity shot's caption bore little relation to the film.*

trousers, his dark hair licked down, with a nice job lined up for him on *The Frost Report*. A top programme, it was the matrix for shows such as *The Two Ronnies* and *Marty* and, in particular, the pre-*Python* venture, *At last The 1948 Show*.

It was on *The Frost Report* that John first met Michael Palin and Terry Jones, both to become future Pythons and fellow comedy heroes. The show was also home to a brace of Ronnies — Barker and Corbett — working together on TV for the very first time. As Barker tells it in *Ronnie Barker: The Authorised Illustrated Biography*: 'John Cleese was very grand, even then — physically I mean, looking down on the world from up on high. Up there in the clouds, a bit withdrawn and abstracted, with that great Desperate Dan chin.' The sketch that everyone remembers from *The Frost Report* in 1966 was all to do with size. It was based around three Englishmen: one upper class (Cleese), one middle class (Ronnie Barker) and one lower class (Ronnie Corbett). The lines weren't funny as such, but the routine — 'I look up to him', 'I look down on him' — worked like a dream. It became one of the great sketches of the 1960s and a lovely reminder that, status-wise, things hadn't changed much under Harold Wilson, after all.

Cleese was never into political satire, though. At Cambridge he reacted against the idea that a sketch should have anything to say or teach; he just enjoyed making people laugh. *Monty Python* was always fundamentally about silliness. It was subversive, true, but it was never political. There was no agenda, just a determined attack on Weston-super-Mare-esque mundanity

One of the team's chief sources of pleasures in life was irritating people. John was superbly good at it and indeed made a short film called *How To Irritate People* (1967), featuring sketches on the gentle art of annoyance. It is delivered in the form of a training seminar (similar to those management training films that he would go on to make for Video Arts), with John on cracking form as the straight presenter.

There are many ways of irritating people. In one sketch, John demonstrated how over-solicitousness (inspired, no doubt, by his mother) can be most effective. Cleese is in a restaurant with a girlfriend (Connie Booth). He abruptly starts up a frantic barrage of ludicrous over-concern for her well being: 'Are you alright, darling? Would you prefer another table? Shall we swap chairs? Are you sure you're comfortable? Would you rather not eat at all? Let me change tables', and so on and so on. Eventually, driven insane by his enquiries, his girlfriend storms out. Cleese is left with a triumphant, 'That's got rid of her' grin.

Another triumphant success was the sketch about the bored airline pilots,who amuse themselves by making announcements to upset passengers: 'The wings are *not* on fire' — totally Cleesian. The masterstroke involves a hapless passenger going to the lavatory. John waits until the passenger's trousers are down and follows on with a curt: 'Would all passengers please return to their seats *immediately*.' Much of this material would resurface later, suitably adapted, in *Python*.

Connie eventually came over to London and she and John were married in early

Right: As Tim The Enchanterer, in The Holy Grail, *featuring a rare outing for Cleese's Scots accent.*

1968. She bought a Hillman Minx; John already had a Bentley S3. On visits to his parents in Weston he must have looked the bee's knees. They bought a house in Holland Park (to this day, John's natural habitat).

John was rapidly discovering that being poker-faced and bizarre was potentially funnier than singing or being loveable. He would leave the cuddliness to Michael Palin. John, with his shark eyes, slightly simian appearance, startling height — and employing a strangulated voice (which required zero lip movement) — was well on the way to becoming a parody of the barrister he never trained to be. A born lawyer, his verbal armoury meant that he could spot and demolish a logical flaw in an argument from a hundred yards. He didn't have to fake his inquisitorial manner.

There is a sublime moment in *A Fish Called Wanda* in which John plays a barrister who is suspended by his ankles from a window. He manages to apologize to his persecutor for his supposed crime, wholeheartedly and unreservedly in a courtroom manner, despite the circumstances. All this he got from Cambridge.

RELEASE THE PYTHON!

Funny is funny, but *Monty Python* was something new: sublimely, deeply, hernia-threateningly hilarious to every teenager in the country. But there was an 'it' to get. And if you didn't get 'it', then 'it' wasn't for you. 'It' wasn't for those who liked dinner-jacketed comedians doing smut, and 'it' wasn't for the sitcom catch-phrase addicts either.

Monty Python was intended for the starved masses who longed for comedy that— when things got boring — would drop a 16-ton weight on its cast. The Pythons, with their sideburns, Chelsea boots and lavish educations, simply leapt into a gap waiting to be filled. True, British TV in the mid- to late 1960s wasn't without innovative comedy. *That Was The Week That Was* and *The Frost Report* had been pretty sharp. *At Last The 1948 Show* was a prelude to the sort of barking mad sketches that would make up the format for *Python*. But TV itself was hidebound by sitcom format, with Steptoe, Alf Garnett and Hancock its presiding gods.

Left: Basil with the staff of Fawlty Towers. Connie Booth was Cleese's first wife. Prunella Scales' Sybil and Andrew Sachs' Manuel (Qué?) became as popular as Basil himself.

The Pythons worked very hard at being as silly as possible and the nation adored it. There hadn't been a sketch-driven ensemble quite like it before or since. Nobody expected *Python*, just as nobody expected the Spanish Inquisition.

Barry Took, John Cleese and numerous others over the years have claimed they thought the idea up. Basically, nobody now has the faintest idea who started it or why. The point was that for a generation the programme changed the face of laughter in Great Britain.

As for the title, *Owl Stretching Time* was one suggestion. Someone thought the show should be called *The Toad Elevating Moment*. John weighed in with his own personal favourite: *A Horse, A Spoon And A Basin*. Michael Palin thought up *Gwen Dibley's Flying Circus*. They finally settled on *Monty Python's Flying Circus*, a title which sounded as if Baron von Richthofen's air team had been signed up by a dodgy seaside impresario. The 'circus' bit harked back to the team's roots in the *Cambridge Circus* university revue.

The rest of the Pythons came via *Do Not Adjust Your Set*, a children's TV programme which featured Eric Idle, Michael Palin, Terry Jones and David Jason. It became cult viewing for adults, who shifted the nation's youth off the sofa in their keenness to see it. Three members of the *Do Not...* team now joined up with Chapman and Cleese, and the sextet were quickly commissioned to write a thirteen-episode series. *Monty Python's* first show went out on 5 October 1969. It was one small step for the BBC, one giant leap for light entertainment. Little was John to know that his legs were soon to become world-famous.

Cleese's pre-marriage flat near Harrods in Knightsbridge, London, became the joke workshop. Sketches burst out of these sessions like roses from Terry Gilliam's animated heads. Cleese was keen on getting the internal logic of sketches right — that Cambridge thing again. Some of the material came from real life. Marty Feldman, for instance, told Cleese he knew of someone who swore he had seen, at dawn, two policemen holding hands on the beat. It was an irresistibly delicious image and the 'Do you want to come back to my place?' copper sketch was improvized around it.

Other sketches came out of what were committee-based, democratic meetings, with Cleese emerging as first among equals. John always laughed loudest. His lips hardly moved and a curious asthmatic wheeze emerged that would be used to brilliant effect in his comedy career. Looking back now, the writing partnerships of Terry/Michael and John/Graham were markedly different in style. Indeed, they were so different that John claimed they used to write parodies of each other's material: 'Terry and Michael's sketches tended to start with long pans over the countryside with maybe a viking — very visual, almost lyrical. Our sketches consisted of people coming on and abusing each other from thesauruses. Graham and I found abuse very, very funny and we loved people arguing, fighting and being rude to each other.'

It was always going to be wacky. The show usually started in the same way, though the credits might not appear until the middle of it. Palin devised the hermit with long, matted hair (like Ben Gunn from *Treasure Island*), who would be seen in the distance, struggling across obstacles on some remote landscape towards camera, just to announce: 'It's...'. Very Michael Palin. John would then announce the title over the programme's signature tune — Souza's *Liberty Bell March* — which would be terminated by the cartoon foot and a squelch.

This was no situation comedy, nor was it family viewing in the way that, say, Morecambe and Wise were. This was different. Parents would sit there with 'I'm-Not-Sure-This-Is-Funny' expressions while the show's younger, target audience simply lapped it up. And if the material wasn't up to scratch, well there was always next week to look forward to. The show became a national weekly fix for a post-*Goons* generation, who wanted a show they could call their own.

SKETCHES OF HEAVEN

Early episodes of *Python* were full of now-famous items: everything from disgusting selections of chocolates (ram's bladder cup and crunchy frog) to ovine aviation. Lines such as 'That's a depressing prospect for an ambitious sheep' would become stock phrases forsenior schoolboys. Large helpings of chartered accountancy, Hell's Grannies terrorizing high streets, men in pubs nudge-nudging, and unexpected visits from the Spanish Inquisition were packed into the menu.

Only *Python's* sense of the ludicrous could come up with a medieval torture in which the victim was poked with soft cushions and had to endure a spell in a comfy chair with only a cup of tea at about eleven.

A lot of the material now seems dated, but when you think about two old ladies (played by Cleese) shrilly discussing their holidays with Jean Paul Sartre in a laundrette, the show still seems unbelievably original. If stuck for a punchline, or when a sketch became boring, they apologized. Continuity links were provided by a sober-faced Cleese in a dinner jacket at a desk (though the desk might be in a lion's cage, or on the beach at low tide, or rotating over a fire on a spit), announcing: 'And now for something completely different.' 'Zany' was the phrase usually — and somewhat inadequately — used to describe *Python* in TV listings of the time. The programme took apart those tired BBC conventions while simultaneously giving the corporation a cult hit.

In the 1960s John discovered the philosophy of Henri Bergson, a Frenchman of Irish-Jewish descent and thus more than qualified to analyse jokes. Legend has it that one day, when Bergson was 25 years old, he went for a walk in Clemont-Ferrand which had far-reaching repercussions. Descartes had made philosophical history with the phrase: '*Je suis une chose qui pense*' ('I am a thing which thinks'). During the course of his walk, Bergson evolved a refinement of Descartes' declaration, which he expressed as '*Je suis une chose qui dure*' ('I am a thing which continues'). He could afford to finish the walk with a smug grin of satisfaction, having in a single phrase altered the course of Western philosophy. But Bergson didn't leave it there. He went on to look at the cause of the human chuckle in an essay of 1911, entitled *Le Rire* ('Laughter'). John read it avidly and it gave him an intellectual basis for the *Pythons'* attack on normality. It also gave him a way of talking theoretically about his work in interviews, disappointing those who expected him to play the twit.

The Bergsonian view was that human behaviour was a rum old business and that laughter was social, a group thing. People laughing at one table over a joke will never amuse people at the next table. Unless, of course, the former table catches fire and the joke is reversed onto the group making all the noise, in which case the social unit expands to fill the entire restaurant. Something like that, anyway.

Bergsonian thinking also came up with the idea that it is 'inelastic' behaviour

Right: The definitive shot of the hotelier from hell. Cleese took great trouble with Basil's all-tweed wardrobe. The cravat was a nice touch.

A loving tête à tête. Sybil and Basil discuss the finer points of hotel-keeping.

which is the source of so much comedy. The philosopher didn't have the benefit of television sitcom by which to test his theories, so most of his thinking on the subject of laughter would have been made with the stereotyped characters of French stage farce in mind. His point was that rigidity, inflexible and unadaptable behaviour tends to be punished with laughter.

A similar premise lay behind *Python*. So much of the humour in the shows is built around colonels, pet-owners, stockbrokers and shop customers desperately trying to retain their sanity in the face of insolence or appalling service. And Bergson's theory certainly holds true for Mr Stimpson, the headmaster John played in the film, *Clockwise*, whose attempts to get to a conference after missing a train result in a day of spiralling disasters.

Anger was a chief tool in John's armoury. Take the sketch in which, as an architect, he shows off a model for a block of flats to some councillors. It becomes apparent that, as part of the plan, provisions have been made for tenants to be slaughtered in a state-of-the-art abattoir. Unsurprisingly, the councillors (they are all freemasons, of course) reject his plan. The architect duly turns from open-faced reasonableness to magnificent vituperation, ending in abject grovelling to have his scheme accepted.

You get more of the same when Cleese turns in his memorable performance as a psychotic chef hurling abuse at some customers ('You vicious, quibbling bastards!'), who had very politely complained about a dirty fork. In a *pièce de résistance*, the chef then kills himself at the table. The trick — repeatedly used in the *Python* shows — was to have the reaction out of all proportion to the situation.

The team's distinct personalities were evident from the first series. Chapman would play ruminative pipe-smoking types and indignant colonels. Terry Jones, a Welshman, specialized in old ladies, clasping a handbag to his chest and shrieking. Michael Palin excelled as brylcreemed spivs, head waiters and shop counter assistants. The cherubic Eric Idle was an expert at doing bouffant-haired TV presenters, his head cocked in mock earnestness. Carol Cleveland —known as Carol Cleavage — just stood around in her underwear in sketches requiring a semi-naked female presence, infuriating feminists who, nevertheless, didn't dare to attack such radical new comedy.

Cleese played tight-lipped businessmen, public information officers, complainants and anyone tall. He always resembled a solicitor ill at ease with silliness, something he had in common with Ronnie Barker. Even when sketches weren't funny — and the *Python* failure rate was, in retrospect, alarmingly high — Cleese was utterly reliable. His ramrod posture, long sideburns, pasted-down hair and the sheer oddness of his shape singled him out as the one who gave *Python* its deeply British and urbane streak, and his rudeness was frequently tempered by a sense of purely professional candour.

Watch him (in stripy T-shirt and mask) robbing what he believes to be a bank. The man behind the counter explains that, in fact, he has entered a lingerie shop. 'No piles of banknotes, then?' Cleese's robber asks politely. Discovering the heist is not going his way, he mutters to himself: 'Adopt, adapt and improve', as if conducting a self-help seminar for those awkward managerial situations. Pure Cleese, pure *Python*.

It was for Mr Teabags at the Ministry For Silly Walks that John Cleese first became known, though. The Ministry devoted itself to promoting and funding novelty gaits of all sorts, led by Cleese, whose own walk to the office was practically a demonstration of government policy in action. Bowler-hatted, briefcase rigidly by his side, feet flicking into the air like pin-striped celery designed by Ronald Searle, he was sublime. But it was a sketch he would come to loathe later on.

The trouble was that John saw himself, above all, as a comic writer and somehow his name became associated with what was, in effect, just a slapstick routine (it had been written by Palin and Jones after Cleese's own sketch about a Ministry of Anger was junked). It was a bit too much for John, and he subsequently became very stingy about requests to see his silly walk. Basil Fawlty, however, would eventually reprise the routine to devastating effect as he goose-stepped in front of some visiting Germans. Well, as Basil would explain, they started it.

GETTING IT RIGHT

Silliness had been seen as a serious condemnation of character in Jane Austen's day, and so it remained in the schools at which the Pythons were educated. By the 1970s, though, the team had turned silliness into a TV virtue. When children are silly it's a bore and you smack them, but when adults in pin-striped suits are being silly, well then you are into Bergsonian country.

John always maintained that he could be funny, but only if he was given enough time: 'I've got quite a logical mind — I was quite good at science and law,' he said on the *South Bank Show*. 'This has given me, in the past, the ability to get the structure of things right. When I first met dear Marty Feldman he went on at great length about what he called the "internal logic" of a sketch, which is that you could have everybody dressed as carrots in a sketch, but if somebody comes in not dressed as a

Right: Cleese as the punctuality-obsessed headmaster in Clockwise *(1986). The film was not a great success, but it gave him the chance to reprise his Basil-ish frustration act.*

carrot, then you have to explain why not.'

The series reflected the anti-authoritarian spirit of the day and managed to hint that something was essentially wrong with British life without ever being specific about it. John later claimed that the series reflected a general dissatisfaction: 'We all feel strongly the world is in a mess,' he told a magazine during the last series in 1974. But if *Monty Python* had a political point to make, it was lost amid the laughter.

The *Python* sketch that was to become most famous was, without doubt, 'Dead Parrot'. It has been ruined by cloth-eared repetitions ever since, but watch it again and it stands up as a mighty comedy classic. Cleese comes into a pet shop wearing a tight plastic mac which is buttoned up to the neck, and carrying a birdcage containing a stuffed parrot. He stands, wearily patient, as the salesman (Palin, of course) insists there is still life in the bird ('It's restin'). Cleese was never finer and the fact that he was prepared to stand there and debate the obviously deceased parrot's medical status added to the cumulative comedic bliss and turned the joke onto the salesman.

The item — like a lot of *Python* material — rested on reiteration and emphasis: 'Now that's what I call a dead parrot' was the trump card in a sketch of quite exquisite Palin/Cleese symmetry. Later on, Lady Thatcher — a surprise fan — famously invoked the sketch to describe the SDP's bird logo. Somehow she wasn't as funny. The *Sun* newspaper revived the joke in 1998 to describe the dead-as-a-doornail condition of William Hague's Conservative party (still not funny). But after *Python*, proverbially speaking, parrots had replaced doornails.

There were several identifiable elements to John's comic make-up. One of them was mascara: he was quite superb at female impersonators. As the mature girlfriend of the terrifying Dinsdale Pirahna (a spoof documentary about the Kray twins), he gave a bar-room monologue in a large orangey-brown wig, in posh falsetto tones that came across not just as funny, but as first-class comic acting.

In another, now largely forgotten, part, Cleese played the head of Allied Bomber Command, Sir Norman 'kill the Japs' Foster. Instead of the moustachioed, no-nonsense senior officer we expect, the camera cuts instead to Cleese in an off-the-shoulder gown, wearing a huge wig and dangling his hand in camp-as-you-like queeniness: 'Hello sailors, guess what? The Ministerette of Aviation has made me head of the RAF-ola-pola!... David Hockney's going to design the bombs.'

Left: The co-author of two of the most successful self-help books written. The therapy-with-jokes format proved a market beater.

The sketch lasted under thirty seconds but it remains a throwaway masterpiece.

Pin-striped types would frequently pop up on screen and make daft announcements. John was great at these too and delivered them in unsmiling tones of utter seriousness with a hint of mania: 'I would cut off the more disreputable parts of the body and use the space for playing fields' — that sort of thing. You have to remember that no-one had ever seen or heard this sort of stuff before. The challenge was to keep it going.

The first *Python* series was good enough to warrant a second, which went out in September 1970 and made the Pythons look rather like schoolboys who couldn't resist baiting a teacher. The first series contained little that would cause any real alarm, but then came one celebrated skit in which John arrived with his dead mother in a sack at the undertakers. Graham Chapman (playing the undertaker) discusses various methods of disposal before coming up with a novel recycling solution: 'Why not cook her up with French fries, broccoli, horseradish sauce?' However, it was the punchline that stuck in the throat: 'If you feel guilty about it after eating her, you could dig a grave and throw up in it.'

The sketch plunged into fresh depths of bad taste and went out in modified form with mock audience outrage cleverly simulated. Jonathan Margolis, in his excellent biography, *Cleese Encounters*, suggests this sketch — and others — were aimed not at the public at large, but at Cleese and Chapman's respective mothers. Back in Weston, quite what the loving Muriel thought of being bagged up and posthumously cannibalized by her own son was anyone's guess. John could be as naughty as he liked on air, but she still wasn't going to let him go out without his woolly on.

A *Python* film was inevitable and it duly came out in 1971. *And Now For Something Completely Different* was cheaply shot and simply packaged up the best sketches from the early series. 'Upper Class Twit Of The Year', flirting once more with bad taste, was one of the most memorable. The film was not a success at the time, and the Pythons made practically nothing from it. The *Big Red Book* (the cover was blue, of course), which was released around the same time, was much better.

Nothing lasts forever, of course. The second series of *Python* had its moments, but divisions in the group were already beginning to emerge. Later, in a 1986 TV interview he said that 'there was a lot of anger in all of us, a fair amount of paranoia

The sedate Hollywood Bowl in Los Angeles was turned into an arena of mayhem for the Pythons' Live At The Hollywood Bowl gig. Palin's socks were declared illegal at customs.

in the group and plenty of envy because we never talked about anything any of us did outside the group. It was kind of taboo. I tried to break it a few years ago by deliberately, in front of everyone else, asking people, "What've you been doing?" So there was a lot of emotion and I think we felt we could have fun with it and, to some extent, make it less frightening by laughing at it.'

In fact, the long and short of it was that John was quickly becoming fed up with *Python*. The money was bad, the timetable unrelenting and, inevitably, the team was beginning to fall out. John's daughter had been born in 1971 and soon afterwards he founded Video Arts, the training film company that would, by the 1980s, be worth millions. More than any of the other Pythons, he had fingers in different pies. Cleese was always being castigated for his business sense by the others and, out of the whole group, it was he who showed the most Thatcherite instincts.

By 1973 the BBC had cottoned on to the fact that *Python's* delight in cartoon nudity meant that the programme could be construed as mildly offensive. Mary

Whitehouse was in on the act, but the series never really suffered from censorship as much as the team would have liked it to have done. Then going through a phase of avuncular liberalism, the BBC seemed to have turned a blind eye to it.

The BBC wanted a third, and then a fourth series of *Python*. By then, Cleese, fed up with being told to turn up at Wakefield station at 8 a.m. on Monday morning dressed as a penguin, had had enough. He quit and the Beeb very nearly cancelled the series. There's no point in pretending that the fourth series was any good. The only thing you really notice is Cleese's absence and the group realized that the game was up. *Python*, after forty-five programmes, finally expired in December 1974. The gorgeous, squawking parrot had finally fallen from its perch and joined the choir invisible.

Not The Nine O'Clock News and *The Fast Show* would later acknowledge the trail blazed by *Python*. John, in turn, doffed his hat to Spike Milligan's ground-breakingly mad series, *Q5*. But like *Q5, Python* was never part of the so-called satire boom. If there was a satirical note in a sketch, a sign would generally flash up on-screen saying 'SATIRE'. What the team excelled at was parody. John's feel for the absurdities of early 1970s television was absolutely spot on. For fans of the Pythons, it became impossible not to laugh whenever a serious news or current affairs programme came on. With Cleese in mind, you waited for the anchor man to say 'And now for something completely different… ' The team sabotaged serious current affairs coverage for a whole generation, much as Chris Morris's *The Day Today* was to do in the 1990s.

During the *Python* years John emerged as a performer as much as a writer, though he insisted he was nothing without a script. This was not quite true since he ad-libbed happily in *I'm Sorry I'll Read That Again (ISIRTA)*, the wonderful, long-running radio series. It kicked off as a pilot show in 1963 and was full of bad puns, songs and material written by regular contributors Graeme Garden and Bill Oddie. John performed frequently on the programme, along with David Hatch and Jo Kendall. He was confident — and starry — enough to have a clause inserted into his contract which exempted him from attending rehearsals, and he remained with the series even after leaving *Python*.

The one thing that emerged from *ISIRTA* was John's ongoing obsession with rodents. His song 'I've Got A Ferret Sticking Up My Nose' — to the tune of 'Rose of

England' — is a memorable souvenir from the series. Indeed, for the twenty-fifth anniversary of *ISIRTA* in 1988, John returned on great form. He attacked his chum, Michael Palin's series, *Around The World In 80 Days*, had a go at his own Video Arts training film and, of course, sang the ferret song.

But for him, radio was different to TV. John remained with the series through thick and thin, perhaps out of a loyalty he had never quite felt towards the *Python* TV project. Typically, it was John who was the first to recognize that *Python* had come to the end of its natural life and, unlike the others, he wasn't scared of the future. For a generation of young viewers, *Python* had, in the words of George Harrison, 'made life worth living'.

John, in the meantime, had a hotel up his sleeve.

GRAIL

By the second half of the 1970s John Cleese's face was as famous as that of President Nixon. *Fawlty Towers* proved a ratings knockout and *Monty Python* had, by that time, become a cult hit across the Atlantic ever since being aired on America's PBS station in 1974. Magazines in the States declared that a *Monty Py-thon* (the emphasis irritatingly on the last syllable) craze was sweeping over the country.

Given that a large chunk of British viewers found the Pythons' brand of comedy inscrutable, it's hard to understand just what the American audiences saw in such a quintessentially English show. Maybe they didn't actually get *Python*, but they still laughed, and provided the team with an overseas market.

John was amazed at the reactions the team got when they performed a series of gigs at the Hollywood Bowl in 1980. He only had to walk on and say 'I wish to register a complaint' and the audience would chant the 'Parrot' sketch, and even the more obscure sketches, back at him as if they were at some religious ceremony. The gig, originally intended as a cash earner, ended up being filmed as a greatest hits package, with the sextet recorded for posterity in their finest plumage.

In the 1970s there was almost something of the cult appeal of a rock group about

Cleese as Reg, the charismatic leader of the Judaean People's Popular Front, in The Life Of Brian *(1983), the most popular film the Pythons ever made.*

the Pythons and they branched into feature movies in the same way that
The Beatles did. In 1975 *Monty Python And The Holy Grail*, the first true Python film
(*And Now For Something Completely Different* from 1971 was really a TV spin-off)
reunited the lads for the first time since John had quit the TV series. He had never
wanted to make the film, but the promise of large quantities of cash (not

forthcoming, as it turned out) persuaded him. Now Terry Jones and Michael Palin had written a new movie, leaving John unenthusiastic but prepared to play a series of parts while Terrys Jones and Gilliam directed.

Totally true to the spirit of the team's comedy, it was a daft, historic, dung-covered 'Carry On up the Dark Ages'. The greatest achievement of the film, which was as blissfully funny as anything they subsequently filmed, was to get the rancid, warty qualities of the period off to a tee, arguably for the first time in British cinema. There had been dozens of Dark Age dramas on screen, but they were usually ridiculous whiter-than-white affairs with damsels and cardboard Camelots.

...*The Holy Grail* was silly, but it shows a curious respect for the period while never losing the opportunity for a cheap gag, innuendo or a song with a bad rhyme (eg 'Camelot' with 'I get to push the pram a lot'). The original idea for the storyline had been for Arthur and his knights to go down to the Grail Hall at Harrods (which has everything) and to buy one. They scrapped that plan and decided to make the film entirely medieval. The sole exceptions to this were the inclusion of a rather unfunny parody on historical documentaries which crops up between scenes — John Young was the on-screen historian — and a squad of policemen who abruptly wind up the film by arresting all the knights.

Apart from about twenty mildly boring minutes, there's a bumper crop of glorious material in the film. In this case, a tight budget became a virtue. The knights seek the Grail without horses, resorting instead to coconut halves banged together for sound effects. Keen-eared viewers enjoyed lines which parodied the stilted dialogue of Arthurian movies. 'This new learning amazes me, Sir Bedevere. Tell me once again how we know the earth to be banana-shaped.' The world of Malory and Chaucer was lovingly revisited, but with much smuttiness (Chaucer would have approved), a large dash of farce and some first-rate verbal insults. And, of course, the knights who say 'Ni!'

The backing came from theatre impresario Michael (*Rocky Horror Show*) White and Led Zeppelin and Pink Floyd were among a handful of groups who invested in the film. However, the Scottish Department of Environment, smelling a rat, were resolutely unhelpful in providing locations, knowing (rightly) that the Pythons would undermine the dignity of their heritage.

But the crew found various locations — Doune Castle was used, along with

AND NOW FOR SOMETHING COMPLETELY DIFFERENT

various wild and woolly bits of Perthshire — and shooting went ahead. For fans of the TV series, the various characters in the film were based on the characters in the show. Graham Chapman, for example, played King Arthur in a way that was an extension of his blustery colonel in the *Python* series. Idle was the terrified Sir Robin and Palin the likeable, bold Sir Galahad, with a cheeriness reminiscent of Jim Dale. Jones played Sir Bedevere, the scholarly one (a nice reflection of his genuine academic interest in the period).

Cleese landed a fistful of roles. His middle-class ferocity was perfect for the ultra-violent Sir Lancelot the Brave, butchering everything in sight and then muttering 'Sorry'. He assumed a wild, Gallic accent for the French knight who waves his bottom at King Arthur from on high and delivers some exquisitely bizarre insults — 'Your mother was a hamster and your father smelt of elderberries' — in a surreal bout of English-baiting. John also played Tim the Enchanterer, a horned mystic who rolls his r's like a Scottish Donald Sinden and warns the knights that the little white bunny rabbit blocking their way has a vicious streak a mile wide.

Cleese also turns in a surreal performance as the Black Knight who, despite having his limbs chopped off, fights on against Arthur while firing off sarcastic taunts and protesting that 'It's only a flesh wound'. The scene was a re-run of the Pythons' infamous blood-soaked 'Salad Days' sketch, and it worked a treat. John adored sketches that involved gratuitous quantities of Kensington gore. He also produced a little cameo as a moronic peasant, whose blood lust — 'Burn the witch!' — contorts his face into a parade of manic Gumby-like expressions. The leather skullcap he sported set off his rolling eyes perfectly, making for a truly alarming sight.

The actual filming was ghastly. Everyone argued constantly, the low budget meant endless discomfort and the technical crew very nearly mutinied. The cast spent miserable hours sitting around in sodden string chainmail and uncomfortable helmets. Graham Chapman's drinking had become so bad he couldn't get his armour on because of the shakes. For the first and last time in his life, John bottled out of a stunt. He refused to run across the Bridge of Death Over The Gorge Of Eternal Peril, a feat that he reckoned required proper footwear and more Dutch courage than even Graham could provide. A mountaineer was eventually called in as his double and strolled across the bridge effortlessly, much to John's

Graham Chapman as Biggus Dickus with John Cleese as the Centurion of the Yard.

embarrassment. He recovered his nerve though, years later, in *A Fish Called Wanda* when, five floors up, he was suspended upside-down out of a window. His face was a vision of perfect calm.

The Holy Grail came out to great acclaim, and proved to be the Pythons' first major success away from the BBC. For reasons undiscovered, it did good business in Russia and in the States, where the team flew out to promote it. Elvis Presley bought a private copy and apparently watched it five times in a row down at Gracelands. The record of the film quickly followed.

But the movie left a nasty taste as well. Team morale was low and mutual

---

Overleaf: Cleese as the waiter whose offer of a wafer thin mint causes the massive Mr Creoste (Terry Jones) to explode in a magnificent shower of sick. The sketch suited John's penchant for the tasteless.

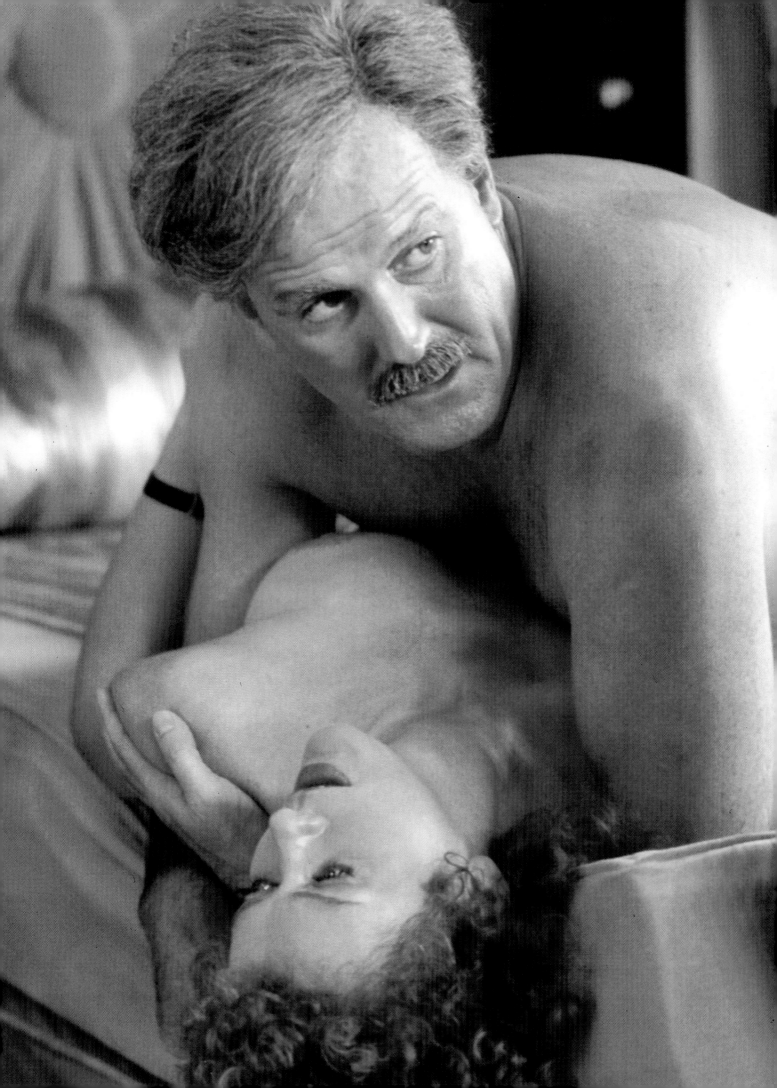

suspicions were growing. One always had the notion that it was John who was the most obvious capitalist in a group that nurtured broadly left-wing credentials. His financial nous and his lucrative Video Arts training films — set up in 1975 and eventually responsible for over 100 films, many shot with old chums such as Tim Brooke-Taylor and Graeme Garden — were resented by the rest of the Pythons. Although John had had no interest in making the last *Python* series, he was the one who wanted to tour live in America, where there was ready cash. At least, that's how the others saw it. The reality was that Cleese was the most distinctive of the group and the most bankable and business-like character. One story tells how he fell over laughing — literally — when his agent told him that Sony were going to offer him a £100,000 advertising contract.

FILTHY TOWELS

L ife outside the *Python* group became an imperative for John. Things get forgotten, contributions overlooked, so much so that nowadays none of the team can now agree on who first thought up *Monty Python*. With *Fawlty Towers*, there was never any doubt. It was John and Connie's creation, their baby. John was bored with writing and performing sketches in which he didn't really believe. The *Python* team was full of problems and John had had enough. He once compared *Python* to walking through a field of unpicked flowers, but the jokes had become repetitive for him and he needed a fresh challenge.

Above all, John wanted to work with Connie. The fact that *Fawlty Towers* was written while their marriage was falling to bits was, oddly enough, not a hindrance. They didn't split up until after the first series, though they were already living apart. Still, their double-act was surely the most successful man-and-wife script for a man-and-wife comedy that has ever been created. Musicals and comedies are traditionally partnership things, the products of professional marriages between like minds.

As was later suggested in the Press, *Fawlty Towers* was a major contributory factor

Left: Pay attention at the back! The sex education sketch
performed in front of bored schoolboys in The Meaning Of Life
(1983). Patricia Quinn played the wife to Cleese's headmaster.

to the Cleeses' separation. Ironically, in many ways it was a happy time and never a word was written unless the two were in the same room together. Both have very fond memories of literally crying with laughter as they bashed out the scripts.

It all started with a typically Cleesian fascination with bad service. Indeed, one of the most delightful things about Basil Fawlty is that he actually existed. He was modelled on a Mr Sinclair, who ran the Gleneagles hotel in Torquay, where John once stayed with the *Python* team. Sinclair was so rude and graceless that the Pythons checked in and then rapidly checked out. Sinclair told Terry Gilliam off for spearing his meat left-handed, 'like an American' (he is an American). 'We don't eat like that in this country' he was informed. When he returned to the hotel, Eric Idle found that his bag had been removed and hidden behind a distant wall in the garden: 'We thought it might be a bomb,' the hotelier explained grumpily, when quizzed. 'Why would anyone want to bomb your hotel?' asked Eric. 'We've had a lot of staff problems lately', came the reply.

John fell in love with this appalling hotelier (and his formidable wife, Mrs Sinclair), for whom guests were a thorn in the flesh. Thrilled with the comic possibilities of such a combination, he wrote the part and tried out his prototype character in an episode of *Doctor In The House* in 1971. Timothy Bateson played a bad-tempered hotelier and the show's producer suggested to John that there might be a series in the character.

The idea stuck and, three years later, John developed it further: 'We saw Basil as someone who was to become a little bit grand, who adopted attitudes of superiority to people that were really quite unjustified, and someone who was fundamentally terrified of his wife. If you look at the episodes, they're almost all fuelled by the fact that he is trying to hide something from Sybil', John explained in an extended interview that came out with the video releases twenty-five years later.

The BBC thought his initial proposal was a non-starter. Even now, there is a framed memo in the Light Entertainment department: 'This is a very boring situation. The script has nothing but very clichéd characters and I cannot see anything but disaster if we go ahead with this.' Can you believe that? At first it looked as though the executive who wrote that memo might have been right. The first batch of *Fawlty Towers* in 1975 got cool reviews and poor viewing figures. There was a general feeling at the BBC that John should never have left *Python*.

Trevor Howard, Terence Stamp and Sean Connery in a still from the lost film, Charge Of The Heavy Brigade. *(Oh alright then. It's Cleese, Palin and Idle.)*

John wasn't helped by the audience for the pilot — 'The Builders'. This is the episode in which Basil employs, in Sybil's words, a thick Irish joke of a builder to rearrange the hotel, and lives to regret it. The show was recorded in front of an audience which included in the front row, for some bizarre reason known only to the powers that be at the BBC, seventy visiting Icelanders from Rekyavik, who watched intently but didn't laugh once. They weren't amused by Manuel or Basil or the sight of the terrifying Sybil beating the world's most useless builder with an umbrella. They simply sat there, silently, and smelling faintly of cod.

Still, the shows (the first series contained six, including 'The Hotel Inspectors' and 'Gourmet Night') were bravely repeated in January the next year. Word of mouth (it soon got around that Cleese was up to something brilliantly original) built up audiences to 7 million, and so it was repeated again, this time on BBC 1, and the audience jumped to 12 million viewers. *Fawlty Towers* was becoming a national obsession. John and Connie were persuaded to write another six episodes for transmission in 1979. When those were subsequently repeated, 15 million folk tuned in gleefully and the show was firmly established as a classic of TV comedy. Deep down in Basil's repressed, irascible, hen-pecked personality, the British people saw something with which they could easily identity and they laughed and laughed at him until the tears rolled down their cheeks.

In TV terms, you could say that Basil Fawlty became Torquay's middle-class answer to Alf Garnett. No doubt, if you had asked Basil why 15 million people watched him, he would probably have tutted something about how his wife, Sybil, 'my little nest of vipers', had managed to put off the other 40 million. Basil was never one to look on the bright side. But the show's sheer comic quality — the result of an absolutely first-rate script — had a lot to do with it.

Ask any comedian, even older ones who often found the manic Cleese persona resistible, and they will all say the same thing: *Fawlty Towers* was as near to comic perfection as it's possible to get in the half-hour format. There has been nothing to beat it, before or since. *Hancock's Half Hour, Steptoe And Son, Till Death Us Do Part, Dad's Army* — all of these shows were golden, but in the end their quality was invariably compromised by quantity. John wrote and starred in just twelve episodes of *Fawlty Towers* and then he quit. What's more, he wrote the series whilst he was going through a prolonged bout of psychotherapy, not to mention the break-up of his marriage. Depression, creativity and laughter: someone really should write a thesis about the combination.

John and Connie got the scripts right through a combination of inspiration and a lot of hard work. Each episode took six weeks to write, an absurdly long time by TV sitcom standards, when ten days was the norm. For every minute on screen they spent one hour editing — an average of twenty-five hours per show. They tweaked, honed, cut and improved the material. John Howard Davies directed the first series, but John and Connie always worked together. It was never just a sitcom. The show's values were essentially theatrical and each episode was a mini-farce.

John claimed that some of the best nights in his life had been spent watching French farces at the National Theatre. A great farce, as any theatre director will tell you, is like a precision instrument. One famous French farce writer was, in fact, an engineer by training. Farces won't work unless you build them — and wind them up — very carefully indeed. John realized that from the start. The Cleeses took an enormous amount of trouble to prevent the audience from guessing the plot, and so they plotted and plotted, wrote and rewrote, and then rewrote the rewrites. Connie was responsible for Sybil; John did Basil. Then they helped each other out with their respective characters, modifying as they went along. To this day John reiterates that it was a partnership. He wasn't being kind: Connie's contribution to the show has always been overlooked.

John took ideas from wherever he found them. For instance, he had a friend — a former employee at the Savoy Hotel — who mentioned that the worst problem the hotel faced was the dead bodies. Guests would frequently die in their beds. In the morning the staff would have to get the body out of the building using the service lift, and without laughing. It was pure, black farce. John lapped this up and used the scenario in the episode, 'The Kipper and the Corpse'. Real life furnished him with all the material he needed.

Overleaf: With Penelope Wilton (left) and Sharon Maiden in Clockwise, *all in varying degrees of desperation. Michael Frayn wrote the script.*

BASIL

John was, of course, Basil, the wild and — a farce word, this — rantipole owner. He was fond of noisy checked tweeds and sarcasm ('It's called "style", dear — you wouldn't understand'). He is also a man teetering on the edge of a massive breakdown. John always considered that the character was very depressed. On the surface, Basil just about manages a prickly politeness. If the guests turn out not to be riff-raff, he assumes an oily smarm. Beneath the clenched exterior, of course, was a seething rage and frustration of the sort John McEnroe would deploy at Wimbledon finals. People go on about Cleese's legs, but the use he makes of his elbows in the first series is striking. They jut out like the useless wings of a flightless bird, especially when he's point scoring or getting a complaint off his chest.

Cleese confessed to Melvyn Bragg that he felt himself, physically, to be a bit of a weirdo: 'I do move oddly. I wish I was a lovely mover, but I'm not. I don't have to exaggerate it much to be Basil. Seeing myself on tape for the first time, I looked like a cross between a giraffe and a hovercraft, as if on an air cushion, with the top half of me waving from side to side. The gestures I made were terribly small and, at the same time, I talked without moving my lips.'

This all came in handy for Basil. John made him in the image of Colonel Blimp. His views on modern art? Socialist. Men with sex appeal? Gladstone and Earl Haig. The Germans? They started it.

'There was an extraordinary emotional reaction we had when we used to think of the things that would happen to Basil,' Cleese said on the *Fawlty Towers* video. 'In a sense we were like gods playing with this man's life and sometimes when we would think of what would happen next, we would howl with laughter and then we would think "Oh, poor man!" Because, as somebody pointed out, comedy is very like tragedy. Henri Bergson said "Comedy requires a momentary anaesthesia of the heart"... We'd laugh first — and then we would feel sorry for him.'

Apart from being a snob, Basil was also very stingy. He was always trying to get things done on the cheap: 'My father was a tiny bit like this,' explained John. 'If Mother had asked him to get some ham he would always come back and she would

Right: Yellowbeard *(1983), the pirate film: Cleese played Blind Pew. He is seen here with Marty Feldman who died on the last day of shooting – a comment on the film, perhaps.*

Dennis Quilley and John Cleese in the much-underrated Privates On Parade *(1982), an adaptation of Peter Nichols' play – Cleese plays the dim but endearing Major Flack.*

say "This isn't the usual ham", and he would say, "No, no, they had some special Norwegian ham this week; they recommended it very highly and said it's better than the ordinary stuff." Obviously it was just cheaper!'

Perhaps the Weston-super-Mare facet of Basil came out in his prudishness and terror of women. And, of course, his almost pathological suspicion of sex. 'The Wedding Party' episode exposed this side of Basil's character wonderfully. A couple breeze into Fawlty Towers, obviously in a state of sexual bliss. Basil, however, regards intercourse as some new-fangled continental activity to be tutted at. But this was the lovely episode in which he himself gets to flirt with the seductive French woman, Madame Penoit, and finds himself way out of his depth. 'You are so charmeeng,' she tells him. 'Only a little,' says Basil, exhaling with embarrassment and gauchely batting his eyelashes.

'People who aren't getting enough sex are fascinated by it,' John explained, when dissecting Basil's character. 'Even if the fascination takes the form of being very, very cross that other people are getting some — and that's obviously Basil's problem. I mean I'm not exactly sure when he and Sybil last did it, but it's a very long time ago, somewhere around the second Punic War, I suspect. I very much enjoy the degree of how he gets worked up. You know, when people say "I'm not a prude but... ", which always means "I am a prude and... ." That episode was an explanation of all that stuff. Basil could never handle anything sexual apart from a little sort of graceful 1920s style flirtation that he can manage quite well and that was probably what attracted Sybil to him in the first place.'

To this day, John remains convinced that Basil is a bastard. He hates him — one reason perhaps why he refused to slip into character in subsequent interviews. 'The thing about Basil, he's an absolutely awful human being. But the strange thing about comedy is that if an awful character makes people laugh — think of W C Fields — people feel affectionate towards them. It's insane because if they had to sit next to him for five minutes at dinner, they would absolutely not be able to cope with him. They would loathe him, but because he makes them laugh, they think deep down he's alright — and he isn't.'

Nonetheless, in Basil Fawlty, John created a sarcastic poet of frustration, embarrassment and good old British guilt. Basil is a wonderfully British comic invention — a liar, a bully, a coward, but above all, a victim.

THE OTHERS

After Basil, Sybil had the most lines in *Fawlty Towers*. If Basil's catch-phrase was a sarcastic 'Thank you so much', Sybil's was the word 'Basil', squawkingly delivered with the promise of some hideous retribution. In the beginning, John wrote most of Basil and Connie most of Sybil and the character that she herself

In Silverado, the only Western Cleese has ever made. He may not be a threat to Clint Eastwood, but the two are at least the same height.

would play, the intelligent maid, Polly — an ironic reflection of her waitressing days in New York. Gradually, they co-operated more and more on all the characters.

With a great stroke of luck John and Connie managed to get Prunella Scales to play Sybil. She, in turn, secured a role which was to make her name. Sybil was always the same — a vulgar, efficient, fag-smoking, golf-playing puff adder, who could read Basil like a book. At first, the couple felt Prunella's interpretation of this hugely competent Torquay shrew wasn't quite what they had in mind. Then they quickly realized that her performance was a vulgar masterpiece: here was a woman who could simultaneously smoke king-sized cigarettes and eat chocolates in bed while reading *Jaws* with her hair in curlers. Prunella also developed the hideous 'uhuhuhuhuhubhu' laugh — John wrote a magnificent line for Basil in which he commented that the laugh sounded like someone machine-gunning a seal.

Of all the characters in *Fawlty Towers*, Sybil is the one who always gets the least sympathy, because she's the only one who is actually in charge of her life — according to her creators' theory. As John says, again on the video, 'you never really minded the things that Basil said to Sybil because she was never hurt by them. There's a certain degree of discomfort that people can tolerate in comedy, but they don't want to see anyone in real pain, or at least not in this kind of comedy. Sybil didn't give a damn, so the insults were fundamentally ineffectual and that's why we could get away with it.'

Oddly, neither Sybil or Basil ever reflect much on their past. Happiness for Basil is a vague memory. Apart from the cock-up over their wedding anniversary, which formed the basis of the episode, 'The Anniversary', we don't know much about their past.

John disapproved of Basil, that 'wretched man' as he would refer to him, but he always adored the Major, a harmless fellow, blazered, boozy, bewildered by almost everything that took place in the hotel, and prone to monologues of sublime nonsense. He was played by the fine character actor Ballard Berkeley — alas, now dead — a cricket-obsessed trouper of the old school with a long career in movies and theatre. The scene in which a stuffed moose head appears to talk (Manuel is unseen below the reception desk, practising his English) and the Major chats to it — well, it's just bliss.

'We loved this guy who was in his own world,' chuckled John. 'He never quite understood what was going on but always added his own insane interpretation of it. Ballard was a wonderful fellow, having had a very distinguished career and it was lovely that right towards the end of it he had this huge hit. I just loved that man. We were a very happy group because everybody was pleased with what they had to do — I can't think of anyone who ever let us down which, when you consider there were eighty people in the series altogether, is astounding.'

But it was always Manuel, with his bandy-legged stagger and his open-faced '¿Qué?', who became in many ways the co-star of the show. After Basil, he was the one that the public latched onto. Manuel was brilliantly played by Andrew Sachs, who gave him a child-like quality, a tan and a 'tache. Basil was forever manhandling, abusing and generally torturing the poor fellow. Manuel's trouble with the English language — 'He's from Barcelona', the explanation which became a catch-phrase — became the show's running joke. When Kurt, the chef, falls in love with Manuel (who rejects him), causing drunken chaos in the kitchen, the situation provided the opportunity for one of just dozens of delightful exchanges:

> **Basil:** This is your fault.
> **Manuel:** ¿Qué?
> **Basil:** You only had to be civil to him.
> **Manuel:** Seville?
> **Basil:** Kind!
> **Manuel:** That not enough. You no understand. He want kiss me.
> **Basil:** Oh, what's one little kiss?

'I can't quite remember how we got to Manuel but I have always found people failing to communicate very funny, from the time I first heard Stanley Unwin when I was 16,' recalled John. 'The joke is not that Manuel speaks bad English but that anyone would inflict him on the general public without training him properly. The terrifying thing is how much children identify with him, poor fellow. Here he is, desperately trying to communicate with a parent figure and getting clipped round the ear for it. It makes you wonder a bit.'

A professional to his fingertips, Sachs suffered dreadfully in the name of art. The blow Basil gave him with a saucepan left him with a headache for two days. When Manuel caught fire in the burning kitchen ('The Germans' episode) he suffered nasty burns, thanks to a lax props department. Acid used to create the smoke seeped through his jacket and reached his skin. The BBC sent him a cheque in compensation. *Fawlty Towers* was a dangerous place to work.

It's been said that Manuel is a racist stereotype who would, these days, never be tolerated. And it's sad, but probably true. But as Andrew Sachs put it: 'If Manuel is insulting to the Spanish, what is Basil to the British?' Besides, when Spanish television bought the series, what did they do? They simply recast Manuel as an Italian.

Right: The line up for A Fish Called Wanda *– co-stars Jamie Lee Curtis, Michael Palin and Kevin Kline, plus a fish, helped make this a bank raid of a film.*

THE GREAT MOMENTS

Where do you start? Was it 'The Kipper And The Corpse', 'Gourmet Night', 'Basil The Rat' or 'The Psychiatrists' episode? Despite the many highlights, it's the dialogue and not the plots in *Fawlty Towers* that you tend to remember. Basil's own stiltedness is a constant treat. Offering two doctors a drink on the house in 'The Psychiatrists', he overdoes the smarm: 'Would you care for a little something with us, a little aperitif, cognac, brandy, on us, with us, which we'll pay for, on the house, as it were?' John poured his gift for ingratiating body language, numbed facial expressions and demented slapstick into the part. It was also first-class comedy acting. Sadly, the National Theatre have still never managed to book him.

One of the great peaks of the series was the car-thrashing incident in 'Gourmet Night' — one of those classic comedy moments on a par with 'The Parrot' sketch. Right at the beginning of the episode, Basil treats his car's persistent vegetative state as an act of gross personal betrayal. Later, on a frantic mission to collect food from a nearby restaurant (Kurt, his own chef, is dead drunk and the guests are waiting for their meals), the car breaks down; it just dies. Basil lets loose a personal tirade at the recalcitrant vehicle: 'I've never liked you, you sonofabitch, you've never run right, you've had it in for me from the beginning, haven't you? Well, you've had it coming to you! I'm going to give you a damn good thrashing.'

Hopping mad, he disappears and returns with a leafy branch from a tree. He proceeds to administer a good flogging to the windshield, with such force that both his feet leave the ground. It's just magnificent. But John believes that the reason the scene is so funny is down to detail: 'No matter how good an idea is, there's always an enormous amount of getting it right technically,' he insisted. 'We tried beating the car with a rigid branch and it wasn't funny at all and so we tried a floppy one — and that didn't work. Finally, we found a branch that had just the right degree of flexibility and it became terribly funny.'

Perhaps the greatest episode of *Fawlty Towers* — at least the one most remembered — was 'The Germans'. It was the show that gained most notoriety and it produced Basil's most famous line: 'Don't mention the War. I did once, but I think I got away with it.' In this episode, a group of polite Germans are staying at the hotel. Basil has concussion, escapes from hospital and tries to supervise their order for dinner in the restaurant. Due to his condition, his unconscious phobias and prejudices come bubbling to the surface. Cleese knew perfectly well that a character like Basil would be quite incapable of thinking of Germans — any Germans — without reference to the Third Reich. The Major, too, thinks all Germans are bad eggs. 'Still, forgive and forget, eh Major?' suggests Basil; then, after an immaculately timed pause, 'though God knows how, the bastards.'

Temporarily deranged, Basil manages to mention the Führer while taking the Germans' order. He then refers to an Eva Prawn cocktail and finally reprises his silly walk, goose-stepping up and down the restaurant, saluting like a Nazi drill sergeant at the Nüremberg Rally, causing tears and misery to his hapless guests and leaving the studio audience helpless with laughter. Ultimately, the scene isn't anti-German at all — more a satire on a particularly buffoonish side to the British character —, but that's how the public saw it. They laughed all the harder as Basil stamped like a bison over the guests' feelings in one of the most politically incorrect moments in modern comedy. As usual, there was an intellectual justification to the scene which Cleese readily explained: 'The point I was trying to make, and this is absolutely true, is that people like Basil are utterly stuck in the past. If you looked at the Germans, all the people he was interacting with are much too young to have had anything to do with the Second World War.'

The scene is about as cruel as it is funny. Years later, John was delighted when he was in Hamburg and a man crossed the lobby of the hotel in which he was staying and said: 'Hey, Mr Cleese. Don't mention ze war.' Still, you could argue that the whole series was worryingly short of the milk of human kindness. The point about *Fawlty Towers* was that, as always, John was determined to move away from the nostalgia, sentiment and whimsy of so much 'safe' British sitcom. He preferred his comedy served near, if not actually on, the knuckle. 'As somebody pointed out years ago, comedy is very like tragedy,' he notes on the video. 'It's just a question of whether you're sympathetic to the people who are suffering or whether you stand back a bit... You have to be a little cool towards the people you are watching. We would laugh at them first, then feel sorry for them after.' And Basil paid for his sins. At Fawlty Towers, sod's law always governed. Basil's fantastically elaborate lies and his recourse to a non-existent war wound in his leg when all his exits were blocked,

was just brilliant. But his ruses never worked. The exaggerated sourness of his ongoing marriage crisis ('Don't drive over any mines, dear') was something Ingmar Bergman would have been proud of. Lurking in the laurel bushes of this sitcom are a lot of uncomfortable truths about the ways in which we deal with each other.

Python had been a comedy of ideas, whereas *Fawlty Towers* is much more a comedy of emotions, mostly rage and embarrassment and British awkwardness at any breach of social convention. It's also superbly gloomy in outlook. Hamlet wandered on stage and wondered whether suicide wasn't the answer. Basil just bangs his head on the reception desk hoping he'll wake up from his nightmare. 'No, it's not a dream, we're stuck with it.'

Basil Fawlty now stalks the hall of comedy fame, along with other great British depressive characters such as Hancock, Steptoe and Garnett and real-life comics such as Spike Milligan, whose comedy was largely influenced by a manic depressive nature. There was talk of a revival and a feature film after the second series. The Americans tried their own version — called *Amanda's By The Sea*; it was, apparently, a disgraceful travesty of the spirit of the original. After show number twelve, John abruptly checked out of Basil's life forever, though John Howard Davies warned him that he would be forever associated with Basil — a prophecy that proved all too true. Would there ever be a follow-up?

The answer was 'Never'. John was adamant about that. Neither he nor Connie felt they could ever top the first twelve shows. The series had come to the end of its natural life and the second series had been a killer — in all, a forty-three week shoot, for which he was paid £9,000. John said on the interview which accompanied the video collection that 'so many people ask me "Are you going to do any more *Fawlty Towers*?" You're up against expectations that could not be matched. The thing is to do something different.'

There was also speculation that the show had finally killed the Cleeses' marriage. This was nonsense. They had, in fact, split in the gap between the two series. John denied it was through pressure of work and Connie has kept quiet about it ever since. John did, however, quote Tom Stoppard by way of an explanation: 'All relationships have a clock attached to them'. However, the legacy of John and Connie's marriage was a show that hit a high watermark in British comedy. If the colours now look pasty and the sets wobbly, the thing that keeps it still fresh is its

Left: Cleese as the lawyer whose hormones play mixed doubles when he meets Jamie Lee Curtis' wily Wanda.

craftsmanship. Well-made things last. John had started the series aged 35, but the price tag attached to it had been a hefty one — depression, divorce (amicable though it was) and a ravenous public who expected him to play Basil wherever he went. People couldn't seem to understand that Basil was a performance, not a person. Worse still, the bunch of attitudes Basil represented and his creator so disapproved of were actually celebrated by his fans.

Basil, of course, would have spluttered 'What is the matter with you people?' and told the general public to get on with their meals. John, though, simply locked Basil in a cupboard, threw away the key and retreated into films and writing psychotherapy manuals. But Basil wouldn't lie down. He cropped up in restaurants and people started to imitate him. In a truly surreal turn of events, restaurants boasting appalling *Fawlty Towers*-style service sprang up. His name is now synonymous with the hotel trade who would rather forget all about him.

HOW TO SURVIVE IT

The 1970s had been a quantum leap for John. Aside from the hotel business, he had married and divorced in 1976 and his adored daughter, Cynthia, was born in 1971. John had gone into psychotherapy and this had even his most loyal fans wondering about him. If comedy is a symptom of something, then cured comics aren't funny. But even his depression was turned to an advantage. He had signed up with Robin Skynner, a fashionable therapist who specialized in cheering up depressed barristers, and formed an unlikely alliance with this woolly jumper-wearing Cornishman between 1974 and 1977. Their discussions provided the basis for the book, *Families And How To Survive Them* and a follow-up title, *Life And How To Survive It*.

What is so strange is that for all their jargon-free common sense, the books — which were subsequently made into a radio series — display Cleese's fascinations with mental health to a most un-English degree. (His third marriage in 1992 to Alyce Faye Eichelberger, a psychotherapist, consolidated his passion for the subject.)

Right: Archie, kit off, is surprised by
unwanted guests in A Fish Called Wanda.

One noted effect of his conversion to analysis in the 1970s was a marked tendency to become rather dull in interviews. But if that was the price of an ongoing genius, then fine. If fans found the families books less than exciting, there was still John's more absurd publication, *The Golden Skits of Wing Commander Murial Volestrangler FRHS and Bar* (Methuen, 1984), to remind them that he was just as funny as ever.

By this time, John could pick and choose his work. Money was heading for his bank account in a steady stream from TV advertisements and from the *Python* series, which meant that he was happy to turn down a proposed collaboration with Abba (who mistakenly thought John Cleese would care to work with them). He took on cameo roles in *The Great Muppet Caper* (John did his familiar upper-class routine) and even appeared in an episode of *Dr Who*. His fans weren't complaining and there was always the prospect of Cleese on the big screen to look forward to. He became a film star, and a very tall one at that. It was a huge relief to all those who felt that he had permanently joined the unfunny farm.

BIRTH OF BRIAN

John rejoined the Pythons for their Hollywood outing. Whatever backbiting and bitching there had been in the group — most of which had calmed down over the years to a low-level rumble — the group's future in films was looking rosy. The team had already thought up their next film before they had even finished ...*The Holy Grail*. It was a short step from Arthurian Romance to the New Testament. When asked what their next film would be, Eric Idle came up with an idea for something big and bold — *Jesus Christ: Lust For Glory*. The others didn't believe this was a serious option.

However, the Gospel according to Brian, the thirteenth apostle, emerged as a viable proposition; some sort of biblical epic appealed to all of the team. The idea of making Brian a disciple was eventually dropped and changed to the story of a half-Roman Jew, who finds himself caught up in historic events in Judaea in 33AD; in other words, a parallel to the story of Jesus. However, the film would exercise the

Left: Wanda's veteran Ealing comedy director
Michael Crichton, with willing student.

Pythons' passion for history and go where no *Carry On* film had dared. The idea of the *Life of Brian* was — as the posters would later claim — to make *Ben Hur* look like an epic.

Backing for the film came from George Harrison, who put in £2 million and released the film through his own recently formed HandMade Films. Now here was an irony of sorts: an ex-Beatle — the band that John Lennon had once famously declared to be more popular than Jesus — funding a movie in which the main character's life bore more than a passing resemblance to that of Christ.

After a team holiday in Barbados (financial hardship was less and less a part of the Pythons' lives) to thrash out the script, they began shooting the film at Monastir, Tunisia in 1978 on the old sets used in Zeffirelli's *Jesus of Nazareth*. The storyline now ran parallel to Jesus' life. In the finished version, Brian Cohen, played by Graham Chapman, is mistakenly hailed as *the* Messiah by a crowd who are desperately seeking any old Messiah. But they pick the wrong one. The deeply reluctant Brian tries to escape from the crowd, gets mixed up in an anti-Roman terrorist group and is eventually cross-examined by the Roman governor (Michael Palin) and crucified. It was decided that John, who originally wanted to play Brian, would take on several parts, since his talents as a character actor were best spread around. He appears in the film as a Wise Man; a Jewish terrorist; a Jewish official and a Roman Centurion.

The film, far from showing up the cracks in the team's ten-year-old plaster, hit a high note and is now considered to be the Pythons' one genuine masterpiece. It exploited *Carry On*-style period gags, it poked fun at *Star Wars*-style excesses and it's main targets were barn door-sized: petty officialdom and religious fanaticism. John Cleese was never better. Along the way the movie — directed superbly by Terry Jones — also managed to lampoon the Bible movies, all of which are unintentionally funny and very American. Nearly all biblical films featured American actors in togas with ethereal music for the religious bits, while the likes of John Wayne and Victor Mature wandered about, looking awestruck. One Bible epic famously opened with the proclamation: 'Men, beware Sodomite patrols'.

Life of Brian broke with tradition in that you actually see Jesus once, right at the start of the film. Played absolutely straight by Ken Colley, he delivers the Sermon on the Mount. Though the historical Jesus was kept out of the movie, except for that

*Right: His hair amazingly in place, Cleese's barrister delivers
a verbose legal apology several storeys up in* Wanda.

opening scene, he had been included in an early drawing-board version of the film. The team all agreed that to have included a portrayal of the real Jesus would have been a dreadful mistake: 'We found that it just didn't work,' said John to Melvyn Bragg. 'Because the moment you got really near the figure of Christ, it really wasn't funny because Christ was wise and flexible and intelligent, and he didn't have any of the things that comedy is about — envy, greed, malice, avarice, lust, stupidity.'

The film's opening pans away from the Sermon on the Mount and on to a bunch of bickering bystanders, listening at the back of the crowd and unable to hear what's going on. The idea that the meek shall inherit the earth is scoffingly met with the general conclusion that it's the meek who are the problem.

The film borrowed scenes from *Ben Hur* and *King of Kings*, and there was also a lovely Shirley Bassey-style Bond theme song for the magnificent opening with Cecil B De Mille-style credits. Jones cast himself as Brian's mother — a raucous pepperpot (a term for the old ladies Jones specialized in playing), who is approached by the Three Wise Men: 'What are you doing creeping round my cowshed at two o'clock in the morning? Doesn't sound very wise to me.'

Cleese, Palin and Chapman were on terrific form throughout. There's a brilliant vignette in which John appears as a Jewish elder, in classic headmaster-style, officiating at a public stoning and sending Eric Idle to the back for throwing his rock before the whistle — 'There's always one, isn't there?' John also took on the role of a Roman Centurian, with more than a touch of an English sergeant major. In one beautiful sequence he catches Brian — a novice terrorist — painting anti-Roman graffiti on the palace walls. Brian has got his Latin grammar wrong and written *'Romanes Eunt Domus'*. The centurion is appalled by his academic sloppiness: 'People called Romans they go it the house', he scoffingly translates, while tweaking Brian's ear.

Cleese's scenes in the presence of Michael Palin's Governor (who is plagued by a terrible lisp and has a friend called Biggus Dickus) are among some of the finest moments of British comedy playing ever committed to film. Palin shone as the transcendentally funny Governor, while Cleese — wearing an expression of wonderful puzzlement — and his Roman cohorts fight a losing battle trying not to laugh whenever their lisping leader opens his mouth.

Then there was Reg, Leader of the People's Front of Judaea, a wonderful Cleesian

Left: John with his old Cambridge chum, Eric Idle.

portrait of petty-minded British trade union belligerence, which John relished. Reg is leader of an anti-imperialist Jewish faction, obsessed with agendas, minutes and meetings. Hatred of the Romans takes second place to hatred of all the other splinter groups. Reg is a definitive study in all-talk-no-action militant union bluster, which gave rise to the 'What Have The Romans Ever Done For Us?' scene, where he tries to remind his brothers of the appalling cost of Roman rule. His question is met by all sorts of cheerful replies, in which the benefits, rather than the curse of the Roman civilization, are itemized, much to Reg's irritated acknowledgement. It's a magical piece of scriptwriting.

The scene at the end of the film in which the crucified Eric Idle leads the singing of 'Always Look On The Bright Side of Life' gave the most offence, and caused even Christian commentators, who could accept the rest of the film, to pause. It was breathtaking in its lack of taste — the final chapter of the greatest story ever told now turned into a blithe, cheery musical number. Was it a parody of the most sacred moment in The Passion? Did it mock Christ for commercial gain? For those not on the *Python* wavelength or opposed to the film, the scene was a hostage to fortune.

Predictably, when the film was released in America in 1979 Christian Evangelist groups, one or two Jewish lobbies and the Southern Bible belt went berserk. The film got an outright ban in two states. In their defence, the Pythons pointed out that crucifixion was a common form of execution in Palestine. Public hanging had been depicted often enough in movies. The argument was logical, if disingenuous. After all, the symbol of the Christian Church wasn't a noose.

John was unruffled by the attacks. If the film had a target then it was false prophets and fanaticism. He argued persuasively that *...Brian* was not mocking Christ. The British censor agreed with him and passed the film uncut. After the London première, Cleese and Palin appeared on the TV chat show, *Friday Night Saturday Morning*, with Malcolm Muggeridge and Mervyn Stockwood, the late (and very camp) Bishop of Southwark.

Cleese himself argued that 400 years ago they would have been burnt at the stake for making *Life of Brian*. The fact that it could be made was surely a social advance of some sort. Muggeridge made a brilliant — and prophetic — point: if the film sent up Islam and Muslim beliefs, he argued, the liberals who supported the film would have utterly condemned it. In the light of the Salman Rushdie fatwa ten years later, the Pythons were, in retrospect, very lucky to have such a tolerant religion to knock.

The debate — chaired by Tim Rice — remains a wonderfully watchable piece of TV. Cleese, freed from the need to entertain, turned his formidable intellectual guns onto the Church Elders. Muggeridge, himself no slouch in the intellectual department, called the film blasphemous and tenth-rate. He asked if it would be remembered in centuries to come like Chartres cathedral? Cleese took the blow on the chin. 'Not a funny building,' he brilliantly countered. It didn't stop the Bishop — who had been playing shamelessly to the gallery — from telling the Pythons that they would surely get their thirty pieces of silver.

Oh dear. It was all very depressing for Michael Palin, the sweetest of men, who couldn't cope with the ire aroused by the film, though in retrospect, what did he expect? John, by contrast, approached the whole thing with relish; it gave him a chance to stop doing silly walks and to get down to some hard-headed reasoning, Cambridge style. He still regards ...*Brian* as the Pythons' finest film, and one of the happiest working experiences of his life. And he also thanks the Anglican Church for all the publicity they generated, helping to turn an art-house film, which no-one would have noticed, into a multi-million pound hit. And though he didn't say it, the film consolidated his reputation. He was now a huge star.

In Great Britain the film, incidentally, had been banned in a part of the West Country, thanks to pressure from the Bishop of Bath and Wells. Was this belated revenge for a delightful *Python* skit in which a family keep putting dead bishops out for dustbin men to collect? Unsure of the diocese of one corpse, Terry Jones squawks: 'Looks a bit Bath and Wells-ish to me.' Down in Weston, John's mother, Muriel, wasn't at all shocked by ...*Brian*. She thought it was a great movie and even helped publicize the film.

The Pythons had licensed themselves as jesters — like the Lords of Misrule in Tudor times — and then mucked about with the stories from the Bible. There wasn't much more to it than that. The film turns religion on its head for a couple of hours, but you sit there enjoying the exercise without being offended — unless, of course, you really want to be. In fact, you could argue that ...*Brian* is not only a very funny film, it's also morally serious in it's own demented way. It brings the absolute bedrock of the Christian faith into the cinema. Brian's one piece of heartfelt philosophy, that 'You've got to think for yourselves', revealed an impatience with

the human preference to believe, rather than to think.

The upshot is that ...*Brian* did great business. The Church turned the other cheek and consoled itself with the knowledge that, in box-office terms, it remains infinitely bigger. In the meantime, the team agreed to make another film and the search was on for a plot.

THE MEANING OF IT ALL

Post-*Life of Brian*, John relaxed into a series of TV commercials and his sole verse role. In 1980 he agreed to make a BBC version of *The Taming Of The Shrew*, to be directed by Jonathan Miller. John hadn't got a lot of time for Shakespeare. He thought his jokes were terrible and he couldn't stand all that cod-piece humour; he regarded him as generally overrated and he hadn't acted in a serious role since his school days. In fact, what he disliked was not so much Shakespeare as the conventions of Shakespearean comedy-playing, with all that motiveless, hearty laughter and thigh-slapping Tudor nonsense.

Miller was an ally in this respect and in John he saw a blend of melancholy and ferocity that was perfectly suited to the part of Petruchio, in the comedy about a prolonged marital row. Shakespeare's Kate, unlike Sybil Fawlty, finally comes to heel. In the video, the bearded Cleese was good, in a muted, downbeat sort of way. But the curse of Basil was still on him. If he wasn't being funny — and he didn't go all–out for laughs in his performance — what was the point of him? Critical reaction was 'mixed'. But John's fans wanted Basil back again. They didn't want to see a comedian being true to a classic text in a serious comedy — which John was.

Typically, John Cleese, the amateur behaviourist, saw Petruchio's vile macho behaviour towards Kate as a form of play-acting, an adopted stance assumed in order to win her love. The play — and his part in it — thus becomes a piercing study in role-playing and this was perfect for him. He came away from the project with a new-found respect for Shakespeare as a psychologist.

The production was good enough to make one regret that Cleese has never been

Left: Cleese's lovelife has usually revolved around Americans. He is seen here with the second Mrs Cleese, Barbara Trentham, and their daughter Camilla.

persuaded back into the theatre to play other parts, including the one bad-tempered, middle-aged role to which he is so suited — Chekhov's appallingly rude Uncle Vanya. John had just one close encounter with Chekhov, back in 1974, when he wrote and co-starred (with Connie) in *Romance With A Double Bass*, a forty-five-minute film based on a short story by the Russian master. But for him, the classical stage remains unconquered territory.

THE MEANING OF LIFE

The Pythons' immediate plan was to cash in on *Life of Brian* and make some big money. Universal Pictures — knowing that by now the *Pythons* were a serious cash cow — came up with the backing. The team had terrible difficulty in thinking up a storyline despite a working holiday, this time in Jamaica. The original idea was that it should be a life story — but who's life? Ultimately, they decided it could be about anybody's life. Eric Idle suggested that it should be about the meaning of life itself. Bingo!

Everyone started writing furiously, with Cleese and Chapman teaming up for an opening number, a birth sequence in a brutal hospital, that marked a return to form. The resulting film — on a massive $80 million budget — ended up as a series of interlinked sketches, a sort of *Seven Ages of Man* retold by nutters. In retrospect, a lot of the material doesn't work; John was always unhappy about it. And in fact, it's perhaps the worst film the team ever made, but it does have some of the funniest things they ever did in it.

The sketch that everyone remembers is the one which revolves around Mr Creosote, a monstrously fat and abusive man in a restaurant, who eats his way through the entire menu, vomits into a bucket and finally explodes in a shower of sick and muck. Hundreds of litres of Campbell's vegetable soup were used for the stunt. Cleese played the servile French waiter, enticing the appalling Mr Creosote (Terry Jones encased inside a vast latex fatbody) to complete his meal with 'just one wafer-thin mint'. The mint causes the final explosion. It was the first attempt to take

Right: The main members of the Fierce Creatures *cast. The animal on Jamie Lee Curtis's lap is a ring-tailed lemur, Cleese's favourite species.*

comedy into an area so gross, so magnificently disgusting, that the sketch instantly became a triumph of excess. Typically, Cleese adored the sketch; the others wanted to leave it out.

John's outstanding contribution was as the headmaster in a sex education scene at a public school. With the aid of his wife (played by the actress Patricia Quinn, now Lady Stephens), he gives the boys a graphic account of human sexual intercourse. What's so lovely about the sketch is that the boys in class — played by the various Pythons — treat the whole episode as if it were some hugely tedious Latin lesson; they look out of the window in boredom, even when the headmaster is stripped, bent over his naked wife and graphically explaining the purpose of foreplay to them.

But the film now stands as a monument to outrage for its own sake, a mixed bag of material that did not possess the communal warmth of either ...*The Holy Grail* or ...*Brian*. It also underlined the hell that teamwork can be. One sketch — a re-enactment of the battle of Rorke's Drift, with Zulus — was shot in the hills near Glasgow and almost caused a mutiny. The black extras understandably objected to the cold and the typecasting; they refused to wear loincloths and walked off. Terry Jones had to find 300 unemployed shipworkers who were prepared to black up. There wasn't enough boot polish to go around, so only their fronts were black. It was a farce.

John — whose grumpiness on set was now attracting the media — got into a fight with the *Sun*, who claimed he had fumed while the extras downed their spears in a storm, shouting, 'Which one of you bastards did a rain dance?' Cleese offered £10,000 to charity if the paper could prove he made the remark. The *Sun* couldn't do so. In a sense *The Meaning Of Life* was the end of an era. It was the last film on which the boys worked together and it was clear that they had finally run out of steam as a comedy unit.

For John, there were filler films to while away the time, plus the ads in which his schoolmaster routine proved useful as a dry run for his role as Mr Stimpson in *Clockwise*. The latter was the next major film he went on to make, and was based on a script by the playwright Michael Frayn. *Clockwise* is a comedy film about a headmaster who makes a mad dash by assorted means, including a pupil's car, to get to a headmaster's conference at the University of Norwich after getting on the

Left: Panic mode in Fierce Creatures*, a cuddly film that bombed despite the film's amazing biodiversity.*

wrong train at the start of the day. In the end, *Clockwise* is an anxiety film about a man having the worst day of his life — a punctual man desperately trying to turn back a tidal wave of setbacks. The film makes great play of deadlines not being met and of loss of control by a man to whom control is all important. His odyssey to Norwich is shared by his pupil (Sharon Maiden), as they drive through countryside, ever more lost and increasingly desperate.

Quite rightly, John abandoned his *Fawlty* persona and reacts beautifully to Frayn's introspective script, inspiring our deepest sympathy. He's superb as the thwarted, disaster-struck, stoical and occasionally funny man whose life has taken a turn for the worse. But the trouble with the film — and this is bad news for a comedy — is that it isn't *that* funny. Probably best filed as an honourable flop, the film taught him some important lessons for his next big project.

However, the movie went down surprisingly well with the public. Radio One listeners voted John, now 48 years old, The Funniest Man In Britain and he even won an *Evening Standard* film award. In his acceptance speech, he later recounted to *Life* magazine, he thanked everybody 'from Soren Kierkegaard to Mamie Eisenhower to The London Symphony Orchestra to my mother, to Donald Duck.'

In the early 1980s John played a series of supporting roles in friends' films. He reunited with Graham Chapman in the disastrous *Yellowbeard*, a rambling pirate romp full of terrible jokes. It was really only worth seeing for Cleese's performance as Blind Pew, a masterpiece of overacting. The part wasn't a job that he particularly wanted, but as a favour to Graham he agreed to it, provided that his part was filmed in a few days and done in England. The cast also included Peter Cook (as a lord) and Marty Feldman — John's old bug-eyed friend from the 1960s — who died on the last day of shooting. The film was dedicated to Marty.

John also appeared in *Privates On Parade*, a HandMade film, based on the Peter Nichols' play and directed by Michael Blakemore, about the British Army song and dance unit in South East Asia (SADUSEA) in 1947. A sort of adult version of the TV series *It Ain't Half Hot Mum*, the film gives a superb insight into the bizarre world of forces entertainment. Cleese played the 'jolly good' British officer, Major Giles Flack (looking not unlike the fruit-obsessed drill sergeant from *Python* and sounding like the Upper-class Twit of the Year). His performance is outstanding, a lovely blend of stupidity and kindness. Major Flack is a prime exponent of the inflexible behaviour

Old pals' act: at the zoo in Fierce Creatures *with Michael Palin and Ronnie Corbett.*

principle through his utter — but never entirely ludicrous — devotion to God and King, and becomes the film's main source of humour and sentiment. Denis Quilley — an actor and former army boxer — took on a drag role, not for the last time.

After *The Meaning of Life*, John was treading water, doing commercials and the odd bit part. He enjoyed acting in *Silverado*, a movie directed by Lawrence Kasdan and shot in New Mexico. This was a straightforward and very long Western with an all-star cast and Cleese in a supporting role as a very English sheriff (seeing him in Wild-West gear is part of the film's attraction). This work introduced him to Kevin Kline — who he would cast in *A Fish Called Wanda* — and enabled him to learn to horse-ride, a pastime that he developed a great affection for. During filming, John overcame his homesickness by reading P G Wodehouse novels.

At home, Cynthia was in her teens and devoted to her father. They had moved into his Holland Park House and enjoyed living there together very much. John's second daughter — to Barbara — was born in 1984, and was called Camilla. The early 1980s had been a busy time for John. He made his first party political

broadcast, for the new Social Democrat party, writing the script himself. His presence guaranteed high ratings as he bored on in a 'quite outstandingly tedious' speech about the merits of proportional representation, in which he repeatedly apologized for being boring. On screen, David Owen gave him the thumbs up. It was embarrassing — but only mildly.

Other broadcasts followed. John was putting his weight behind a political alternative that, years later, Tony Blair would cheekily adopt for himself — the third way. Cleese argued for an improved society along the lines of the self-discovery he had experienced in his therapy groups, advocating a politics of openness to ideas, freedom of information and acknowledgement of mistakes. Politics were not really John's natural habitat, but for those masses left paralysed from the neck upwards by the ghastliness of party politics, he was a breath of fresh air.

The films he worked on at this time were ultimately not satisfactory to him because they weren't his babies. Looking back on the period, he was to tell one reporter: 'I do sometimes think, what did I do in that period? Let's say, 1981–82. Well, I got married to Barbara... I recall writing some rather good radio ads for America, and did some bad movies: *Yellowbeard*, *Privates On Parade*... I tend to do a small number of things, into which I pour inordinate amounts of time. Look at the other Pythons — Terry Jones's CV is stuffed full of things. Mine is more spread out.'

WANDA-LUST

A Fish Called Wanda was to be the big post-*Python* blockbuster. For Cleese, it was the summation of the 1980s and became the most successful British film ever — until, that is, *Four Weddings And A Funeral* (about which John was a bit sniffy) and *The Full Monty* came along. It took a fortune at the box office (£22 million in just the first seven weeks of opening, having cost less than £5 million to make) and its various BAFTA awards and Golden Globe nominations now fill the Cleese trophy cabinet. *A Fish Called Wanda* also made him several million pounds better off (the rest of the principal cast were, happily for them, on a profit share).

Left: With his third wife, the psychoanalyst Alyce Faye Eichelberger, and John's daughter Cynthia.

You have to add that sum to the proceeds from Video Arts, John's training film company, which was sold for a cool £7 million at around the same time. The Press lapped up these financial windfalls: there was a feeling that cash was drenching John like a waterfall and that his Midas touch was now the most interesting thing about him. Cleese told the *Mail On Sunday* that, 'People think I made a fortune when I sold Video Arts. In fact, I made £7 million and was supposed to pay 50 per cent tax on that. If I tell you that my second wife (Babs) got £2.5 million, that I bought the house next door for over £1 million and gave £600,000 to charity, you'll realise that I'm already in the red.'

Easy come, easy go. His old chum Palin was probably doing just as well, if not better, financially. Jonathan Margolis, Palin's biographer, recounts a story that Palin's royalty cheques for his massively popular BBC travel programmes and books were so vast the Director General had to sign them personally. Both comics were now in the British super league. Indeed, there's no arguing about the commercial success of ...*Wanda* as a project, but an artistic question mark hangs over both ...*Wanda* and it's ill-fated follow-up, *Fierce Creatures*.

For one thing the film turned the John Cleese we knew and loved from a comedy actor into a sex god — a dodgy role for a comic who had 'failed bank manager' written all over him. It was partly his own doing. For reasons entirely connected with vanity, and to which he readily owned up, John had already had several hair transplants since the late 1970s. By the time ...*Wanda* was made, he was nearing 50 and, thanks to a French trichologist, it looked as if thin clumps of seaweed had taken reluctant root on his scalp. All those gags about toupees in *Python* (a toupee was regarded throughout the series as possibly the funniest single item on earth and was the subject of one fine sketch, in which Eric Idle sported a large furry rodent on his head) seemed to have made no difference to him.

John also worked on his physique with the aid of a personal trainer, giving his torso a knotty, lumpy look as if he had sprouted biceps on his chest and legs. The reason for this was that he had written himself a scene in which he appears stark naked and had no intention of looking like a 6 foot-plus lump of lard. Yet, from a purely artistic point of view, an athletic frame was quite unnecessary, given that he was playing the part of a middle-aged barrister and many barristers are shapeless, unfit, Rumpole-ish types, not noted for their bronzed, washboard stomachs.

Like John's body, the script, too, underwent endless workouts. The screenplay was composed with the usual Cleesian battery of flow charts and diagrams — his consumption of felt-tipped pens was phenomenal. The screenplay was a massive structural exercise at which he beavered away, just as he did with *Fawlty Towers*. Interestingly, *Four Weddings...* went through over a dozen rewrites before its writer, Richard Curtis, was satisfied, and it is now British film-making lore that a script is perfectible by sheer slog. It was actually only after the film came out that Cleese took himself off to Robert McKee's famous Story Structure Course for aspiring film writers, who learn the craft by analysing scenes from *Casablanca* endlessly. The course was very popular, despite the fact that McKee had had more success in running the course on how-to-do it than by actually doing it himself.

Perhaps the nicest aspect of the entire *...Wanda* enterprise was John's hiring of an old-timer, Charles Crichton, a distinguished Scottish film director who had been making movies since before the war and whom John had recruited for the odd Video Arts film. He wanted a man with experience and, to his credit, he was undeterred by Crichton's age (he was 77 at the time) although it worried the film's producers, MGM.

Crichton had directed, amongst other films, three golden Ealing comedies: *The Lavender Hill Mob, Hue and Cry* and *The Titfield Thunderbolt*. After a gap of twenty-two years, *...Wanda* — an Anglo-American bank heist caper — was to be his comeback. He wasn't the wrong man for the job, but any of the insular Ealing gentleness he may have imparted to the movie was ultimately scuppered by the film's big-budget Hollywood pretensions. Crichton stayed the course despite his back problems.

The idea was to have a starry cast — well, relatively starry. Cleese's love interest was provided by the glamorous Jamie Lee Curtis (daughter of Tony Curtis), known in Hollywood as a 'Scream Queen', having made her mark in the slasher film *Halloween*. She was to play Wanda, one of a gang of robbers which included fellow American, Kevin Kline (Cleese had liked him in *Silverado*), Michael Palin and Tom Georgeson. Other key parts included the excellent Patricia Hayes as the old lady whose pet dogs are executed one by one. The comedy was kept black wherever possible.

Cleese plays Archie Leach, a barrister married in tolerable misery to Maria Aitken. The pair live in their stockbroker-belt mock Tudor home with Portia, their brat of a teenager, played by Cleese's own daughter, Cynthia, who turned out to be brilliant as the snotty, spoilt, pony-riding, Home Counties princess. Not to be outdone, the second Cleese daughter, Camilla, made an appearance — her debut — on her father's shoulders in the video film about the making of ...*Wanda*.

Cleese's own character, Archie, has his role complicated by a love affair, which the Americans wanted central to the plot to balance the blacker side of the comedy. Archie falls deeply in love with Wanda, who eventually elopes with him. Cleese — in an expanded version of the lawyer role he had played a million times before — is effortlessly superb as the pompous, emotionally ossified lawyer whose emotions are re-awoken when he finds romance. But one of the problems with the film is that we are expected to take the romantic content seriously. There is something odd about Cleese's breathy attempt at romantic charm which left a few people thinking that, having borrowed Cary Grant's real name (Archie Leach), he was under the illusion that he was actually Cary Grant reincarnated. John Cleese as a matinee idol? It's a worrying concept and one which the film's ending — Archie and Wanda on the plane to Rio — does nothing to undermine.

But ...*Wanda* has its fair share of vintage moments. Kevin Kline, who won a Best Supporting Actor Oscar (it was admittedly a thin year) for his role as the heavily armed Otto, the Nietzsche-reading, Brit-hating and obtuse accomplice of Wanda, is on fine form. His confrontations with Cleese are consistent fun. One of the highlights of the movie has Archie suspended by Otto upside-down from a 100-ft high Docklands flat window. He is forced to offer Otto a formal apology for insulting him, in legalese, while hanging like a bat. Only Cleese could have thought that up.

The film also took the John Cleese critique of British life to an extreme. It develops a theme on which he had been working for twenty-five years: Englishness as an affliction. But what on earth would Fawlty — who had little truck with Americans — have had to say about Archie's key speech to Wanda: 'Do you have any idea what it's like being English, being so correct all the time, being so stifled by this dread of doing the wrong thing? We are all terrified of embarrassment... That's why we're all dead. Most of my friends are dead, you know we have these piles of corpses to dinner. But you're alive, God bless you.'

When, at the end of the film, Archie unleashes a tirade against Americans, there's some element of payback, but it's altogether less heartfelt. Having two American

Right: The famous Cleese wardrobe includes a lot of dubious woolly jumpers, like this one.

Livening up Paddy Ashdown's election campaign. John supported the party which Margaret Thatcher compared to a dead parrot.

women as wives, John's identity seemed marooned somewhere in the mid-Atlantic. The cultural warfare in the movie — American vigour versus British reserve — is pretty lopsided, since it's American prejudices which are being pandered to. Given the commercial success of the film, it was a well-judged form of pandering. Whatever, the film's level of Brit abuse seems almost masochistic.

Michael Palin, as Ken, the badly-dressed gangster with a curly wig and a chronic stutter (an affliction from which his own father suffered), provided some of the funniest material in the film. Needless to say, a large number of Americans found the film offensive and 'the stuttering community' complained to the producers. Palin and Cleese actually have very little screen time together, which is a shame. But towards the end of the film, Archie, who patiently waits for the stammering Palin to explain the whereabouts of the loot, provides a lovely touch between two old friends, in a film which needed all the lovely touches it could get.

...*Wanda* is shot throughout with strong language, which meant it had no place on the family-viewing shelf and this gives the film a dubious air of American sophistication. It had worked in *Life Of Brian* and yet, for some reason, the number of expletives grate in ...*Wanda*, a film which had no particular need for streetwise realism. Despite moments of brilliance — Cleese in the courtroom scene when he cannot continue a cross-examination in court without saying the word Wanda is delightful — the final impression is one of contrivance.

But these criticisms are not shared by the millions of people who made the movie a monster hit and won it all sort of awards. With ...*Wanda*, John Cleese had finally cracked Hollywood. He was a superstar, even a mega star. Overall, 1988 had been a bumper year for him. The film's 1997 sequel was almost bound to fail, though in the event the press vilification of *Fierce Creatures* was as misplaced as the lavish praise heaped on ...*Wanda*. It was a long time before Cleese returned to film making. The stories surrounding *Fierce Creatures* — one projected title, *Death Fish 2*, was abandoned — started to pile up. The film was never intended to be a sequel to ...*Wanda*, but an extension of it — a film which strove to find a warmth and honesty that had been missing in the earlier outing.

...*Wanda* and *Fierce Creatures* took up ten years of John's life. The period also saw his divorce from Barbara come through in 1990 when Camilla was six. Amicability was preserved, however — Barbara bought a house around the corner. In this case, the marriage seemed to have petered out rather than to have hit any rocks or had any third parties involved and both felt it was time for a new chapter.

Without doubt, the major emotional event for John, other than his marriages, was the death from cancer of his great friend and writing partner, Graham Chapman. His condition had been diagnosed in 1988, the disease spreading to the spine, its progress lovingly charted by the *Sun* newspaper which later — in a rare show of decency — adopted Chapman as its pet cause. Graham died in October 1989, and both Cleese and Palin were at his bedside when he died. Cleese was distraught and wept buckets, as much for Graham's stoicism as for the loss of his bizarre Cambridge friend, with whom he had written all those mad, confrontational sketches in the past. The funeral service was at Bart's hospital. Cleese's eulogy is now famous, since he simply couldn't let his old chum join the choir invisible without a laugh. He spoke of Graham as a deceased parrot — repeating the sketch — and then went on to say what a tragedy it was for everyone. He concluded, in a twist that must have left the vicar breathless, with the assertion that Graham was 'a freeloading bastard, I hope he fries'. Chapman would have loved every minute of it and David Sherlock, Graham's partner for years, approved of the send-off for the first Python to fall from the perch.

John may have been robbed of his writing partner, but he wasn't finished with romance. The fact that Barbara had borne a passing resemblance to Connie was duly noted by various catty pundits when he met his third wife, Alyce Faye Eichelberger (née MacBride), the ex-wife of a Texan golf pro. *Families And How To Survive Them* should really have been titled *Families And How To Swap Them*.

At the time there was a joke that John had married the same woman three times in a row. His new woman was blonde, American and — the crowning glory for John — a shrink. Alyce Faye was a Kleinian/Jungian psychotherapist who worked with adolescents at the Tavistock Centre in London while running a private practice. One day a doctor with whom she worked suggested she might like to meet a friend — John Cleese — at a dinner party. Since Alyce didn't watch TV, she wasn't clued up about the comedian. She agreed to go along to the dinner party on a blind date, provided that there were enough guests so that if she didn't like him, she could always talk to someone else. However, they hit it off immediately. John got her number from the phone book and called her three days later, asking her over to supper with Robin Skynner, the co-author of his therapy books. She was late, only turning up in time for pudding, but John can't have minded too much as they went on to get married — in Barbados in 1992. Having promised that she would be around when he was working, they both walked hand-in-hand into the *Fierce Creatures* project. Alyce was planning a book about mothers and hung around the set while John faced the nightmare of making the film. If there is only one thing worse than a stage musical going wrong, it's when the same thing happens to a movie.

Right: 'Have you met the poor?' John modelled his Robin Hood in Terry Gilliam's Time Bandits *on Prince Charles.*

Pressing the flesh: Robin Hood meets the midget robbers in Time Bandits.

FIERCE CREATURES

There was only one route for the newly married, happy and healthy Cleese. It was just too tempting not to try to make a follow-up to ...*Wanda* and to somehow repeat its chemistry and success. This was a doomed task, but a screenplay was forthcoming, this time written with his journalist friend, Iain Johnstone. The new film — about a zoo threatened with closure if it doesn't make a profit — was all to do with his fascination for friendly, rather than fierce creatures. As a schoolboy, John had fallen in love with a ring-tailed lemur in Bristol Zoo. John, who filmed the movie in part at Gerald Durrell's zoo in Jersey, contacted an expert for a list of the five other cuddliest creatures on the planet. The top five? Wallabies, meerkats, maras and coatimundies. The lemurs would later get a documentary all to themselves.

The cast finally consisted of 115 species of animal. The film itself was dedicated to Durrell, who died — along with Peter Cook — in 1995. It's about a small British zoo that happens to be owned by a nasty conglomerate. A David and Goliath story with added mammals and a cast of pals that saw faces from the old days, notably little Ronnie Corbett in a sea lion suit, as well as reuniting the old ...*Wanda* gang. Cleese cast himself as Rollo Lee, a retired Hong Kong police officer, now working for a multi-national corporation, Octopus, whose mission is to increase the zoo's profits by 20 per cent. Kevin Kline was invited to play the dim son of the Murdoch-like bigwig corporate raider. In a clever stroke of casting, Cleese got Kline to play both the weak son and his appalling father — an ocker ogre, who farts and burps, and is surrounded by 'Yes' men. His death (the son shoots him) is the subject of a cover-up in the last reel.

Jamie Lee Curtis — whose role was purely decorative — was brought in as the zoo's new marketing director, whose steely ambition is softened by the keepers' love for their furry friends. The keepers were led by Michael Palin, again rather wonderful, as the insect lover. But violence is the zoo's business plan. All the non-killer animals have to go. This initiates a deception plan by the rest of the zoo-keepers — Ronnie Corbett, Robert Lindsay, Derek Griffiths and Cynthia Cleese (again) desperately trying to convince Rollo that the animals are lethal.

Rollo, it turns out, has a heart of gold and, instead of shooting the animals, he keeps them in his house — a prime set-up for a lot of sex and animal gags. The zoo gangs up against the wicked capitalist, the father is shot and the rest of the film is taken up with making the death look like suicide. In the dying moments of the film, Rollo — a lovely study by Cleese in ex-patriate decency and pomposity with more than a hint of Basil — calls Willa (Jamie Lee Curtis), 'Wanda'.

The film never sustains the excitement, but it has its fair share of funny moments. It's also a charming defence of all creatures great and small, and by extension, the British way of life, against the ruthlessness of global corporations. In that sense, *Fierce Creatures* comes far closer to the traditions of Ealing than its predecessor. John Cleese assumes a moustache and military bearing; his sexuality is bristling beneath the moustache, but he's British to the core. Never one to forget his friends, the film was stuffed with John's mates from the business, though this time around, Maria Aitken and Tom Georgson played very minor roles.

But although the film started out with plenty of cash backing — it cost £14 million to make — things started to go wrong right from the beginning. Veteran director Robert Young, who years before had directed Polly and John in the nude for *Romance With A Double Bass*, was replaced by Fred Schepisi (an Australian director who had made the Steve Martin film, *Roxanne*), whose idea of comedy was totally different. Almost half the film had to be reshot when it was discovered that a sample audience disliked the ending. The reshoots cost $7 million.

The Press quickly scented failure — a great story after the massive success of *...Wanda* — and a 30-year-old career facing failure for the first time. It was the old story: they build you up, they knock you down. There was very little fun in the making of the film and rumours seeped out that morale was low. Jamie Lee Curtis was not on set enough as she was desperate to get out of scenes so she could see more of her children; Kevin Kline was showing signs of Hollywood-itis, insisting that the corridor outside his dressing room was carpeted so he could sleep better; he remained grumpy throughout the shoot. The directing arrangements were bizarre, too. Cleese gave the cast notes and advised on their line readings, while Robert Young set the cameras up. No-one quite knew who was ultimately in charge of it all.

'The script never relied on obscure jokes I didn't think audiences in middle America would find funny, so there aren't any references to Heidegger,' John told David Gritten on the *Daily Telegraph* in a post-mortem interview. 'We all agreed the ending didn't work. The new ending came from Carla Shamberg — that classic Hollywood figure, the producer's girlfriend and now his wife. It was her idea; it was brilliant... People think I listen to too many opinions, but I listen sceptically.'

Like *...Wanda*, the script came from hard slog. John also told the *Daily Telegraph* that it didn't come naturally: 'I saw Peter Cook being a comic genius for fifteen years. He'd sit there and, as Frank Muir said, saw it off by the yard.' Neither Cleese nor any of the other Pythons could do that. In the same way that John stopped writing *Fawlty Towers*, he knew that he would be unable to improve a follow-up to *...Wanda*: 'When I wrote *...Wanda*, I had no idea what a big hit it would become. I'm beginning to have sympathy for poor Orson Welles, who made *Citizen Kane* when he was 25. What do you do for the rest of your life?'

The comparison with *Citizen Kane*, routinely voted the greatest film ever made, was a bit unfortunate. Pretty soon after *Fierce Creatures* started running into trouble,

Right: 'Get out of my chair, now!' Cleese with HRH Prince Charles in the director's seat.

the *Daily Telegraph* was on the case. An investigative arts reporter, Sue Summers, got hold of an anonymous crew member, who delivered a damning verdict on the whole unhappy enterprise: 'The trouble is that John is so intimidating — because of his size, because of his intellect and because of all the power he wields. Everyone's scared of him and afraid to tell the truth. John is one of the wittiest men I've met, but he doesn't really believe in the things he preaches. I can tell you — he's the last person who should write books on management or family therapy.' Bitterness from anonymous underlings shouldn't be taken too seriously, but as the author and star of the film, Cleese was getting stick from all sides.

Still, the film didn't fail for lack of publicity but the tone of the coverage was nasty. For the first time, John had become a real target: 'It was unpleasant,' he told *The Telegraph*. 'You felt people were celebrating the film's failure in advance. Some reports were almost gleeful. It's not nice sitting around thinking: "Wouldn't it be fun if this fails?" '

But is the film a failure? Not at all, if you judge it in the light of most British films. The trouble was that expectations for any John Cleese film were absurdly high. Still, for fans there is plenty of good-natured comedy, one or two key moments and tons of assorted wildlife. Cleese's Rollo is a fine addition to the collection of Brits — part-character study, part-critique and nowhere near as soppy as Archie Leach.

Judged by the final product, the movie's rewritings seem justified and necessary. In the end, although the film isn't a masterpiece, it's still frame-for-frame funnier than all the other *Pythons* films put together. It is also more fun in its own way than *...Wanda*, though it doesn't have such highlights. The trouble is, movie history doesn't see it that way and the film actually took very little money. It came out in 1997 and was blasted out of the water by the success of Rowan Atkinson's film, *Bean: The Ultimate Disaster Movie*. Bean has replaced Cleese in the Hollywood consciousness as the definition of British humour. *Fierce Creatures* went down like the *Titanic* and it's never coming back up. Sometimes it now crops up as a video, though usually in the discount bin.

TAKING IT EASY

There is a wise saying that young men spend their lives trying to build a bridge to the moon. But then when they reach middle age, they take it to bits and build a shed. With Cleese now just this side of 60, the 1990s have turned out to be his 'shed years', and he has spent a fair amount of time happily pottering about. One of Britain's most successful businessmen, he claims the only question he ever asks his accountant is 'Do I have to work?' and for years now, the answer has been 'No'.

Not proper work, anyway. Money has just seemed to stick to him — even when he wasn't being particularly funny. At the end of the decade, an advertising agency employed him to bawl down a megaphone, Fawlty-fashion, at customers to tell them about low prices. It wasn't funny, the ghost of Basil wasn't summoned and Sainsbury's were not amused. They took the account away from the agency responsible. Still, if he was upset then Cleese must have sobbed all the way to the bank: the grocery chain paid him an estimated £400,000 for the ad.

John's earning capacity may have often irritated his fellow comics. He has never really been interested in politics as politics, but his profile and business acumen have made him important to various parties who would like to have him 'on side'. In his time he has made party political broadcasts for the Social Democrats — the broadcast in 1985 got phenomenal ratings and for a while David Owen was given the nickname 'Basil' in the House of Commons — and for the Liberal Democrats. He has also declared for the Green Party. Cleese has shown admiration for conservative politicians of the wetter variety. Like Martin Bell, he has thought of becoming an MP, but is so horrified at the profession of politics that this seems most unlikely. He regards politicians for the most part as a lot of big kids inflicting their childhood emotional problems on the world.

As for another feature film by and starring Cleese, the unhappy experience of *Fierce Creatures* has probably put him off for good. To him, it is probably much easier to appear in other people's films, take the money and run. Besides, his career has begun to enjoy a generational warp. By the mid-1990s children who had got to know Basil from watching *Fawlty Towers* repeats and video had come to love him, although they love Manuel more, perhaps. But for the under-10s, Cleese is a hero to a new generation of comedy fans unaware of his past *Python* fame.

Cleese has almost become a ubiquitous presence in feature films, having turned himself into a character actor specializing in stuck-up English gentlemen. He remains superb at stiffening the top lip when required and then undermining the stereotype. The high point of this specialism was his cameo in Terry Gilliam's 1981 film *Time Bandits*, in which he played Robin Hood as if he was Prince Charles. The performance was sublime. 'So you're robbers, are you? Jolly good — do you enjoy robbing? The poor are going to be absolutely thrilled. Have you met the poor? I know you'll like them, charming people.' Cleese can do this sort of character-acting brilliantly — and in his sleep; there is no-one to touch him at it.

If he has started to sound like royalty on screen it is through a first-hand connection. Like almost every other comic, he has worked with Prince Charles. The Prince appeared (as himself) with John in a film for charity on business and the environment. Charles was dreadful. Cleese was diplomatically charming about the performance, though in his earlier days he would never have been so merciful.

But the toff parts that he has off to a tee have formed the basis of a large chunk of his career. The Upper Class Twit Of The Year, which he developed for *Python*, was watered down into a serviceable, if bland, cameo. He appeared in the *The Jungle Book* — yet another film version of the Rudyard Kipling work, directed by Stephen Sommers for Disney — which provided him with the opportunity to ride on an elephant wearing a white suit (Cleese, not the elephant) and to give a party of college girls a lecture on lemurs.

In the 1990s John has still got parts as a solicitor. He added a bent lawyer (called Shadgrind) to his long collection of lawyers for Eric Idle's film *Splitting Heirs* (1993), a pretty dire affair in which Eric Sykes and Cleese provide the few laughs on offer.

There's little rhyme or reason to the work he has taken on in the last decade. He was most bizarrely cast, for example, in Kenneth Branagh's earnest film of Mary Shelley's *Frankenstein*, which boasted Robert De Niro, as the monster, sharing the screen with Richard Briers as a peasant — a surreal scenario that not even *Python* could have dreamt up. The film also features Cleese being frightfully dramatic — and intentionally unfunny — in a wig and false teeth as Dr Waldman, the progressive professor who teaches Frankenstein about the possibilities of

The fresh fruit sketch gets a mention in the Disney film, Rudyard Kipling's The Jungle Book.
Lena Headey supplies the crumpet factor.

re-animated life. Frankenstein's parrot springs to mind — but alas never gets a mention — when watching this scene.

In 1998 Cleese made a guest appearance, spread over two episodes, on the phenomenally successful American sitcom *Third Rock From The Sun*. He played opposite the one American actor to bear any similarity to him: John Lithgow. As if to accentuate the irony of the situation, Cleese played a professor, like Lithgow, who is actually from another planet, again like Lithgow. The difference was that Cleese's character hated humans and took full advantage of their soppy, sentimental ways, while Lithgow's character actually loved the mush. For Cleese this was a familiar role, combining the lofty imperialism of *Python* toffs with a little of Archie Leach's

sex appeal (he got a 'love scene' with Lithgow's romantic interest), but adding a genuine dash of dastardliness. It is possibly one of his finest cameos but ultimately it was, well, just work. It meant a bit of extra cash and no long months of filming.

KILLING TIME

When you're a name, albeit a very, very big name, getting your own films off the ground is still a life-threateningly stressful business. It's easier, surely, to relax and to play it by ear. Cleese, who still lives in the Holland Park house that he bought from Bryan Ferry, has become more interested in a way of living than in making a living. Philosophy and psychology remain passions for him and the two books that he wrote with Robin Skynner are regarded by him as among his best and most useful achievements. He remains passionate, too, about business and training, and the psychodynamics of human co-operation.

In 1999 he gave a serious interview to the business magazine *Fortune* on the subject of 'smart managing'. In it, he mentioned a meeting he had once had with the Dalai Lama. It was a typical case of Cleese name-dropping. Can you imagine, say, Tommy Cooper chewing the cud with the top Tibetan?

'I asked him why it is that, in Tibetan Buddhism, they all laugh so much,' said John. 'It's the most delightful thing to be around them because they are constantly in fits of giggles. And he said to me, very seriously, that laughter is very helpful to him in teaching and in political negotiations because when people laugh, it is easier to admit new ideas to their minds.

'Peter Ustinov said that his life really began to take off when he started to do things that really interested him. And as things genuinely intrigued me... I got drawn into them. I think you should let yourself do that. If somebody had said to me in 1966: "You're going to spend thirty years of your life with a management- and sales-training company", I would have said: "What are you talking about?" '

Cleese's campaign against bad management was really his campaign against the work place. Millions of people chained to computer screens, not stopping to think,

---

Left: A bad hair day for Cleese, as the strange Dr. Waldman in Kenneth Branagh's film version of Mary Shelley's Frankenstein.

Overleaf: Putting the pith in Python's The Meaning Of Life: *the team's habit of dressing up as endangered species started back in the pantomime horse sketch.*

is John Cleese's idea of madness. He despises organizations run and fuelled by fear.

As he once said to *Fortune* magazine: 'When people ask me to do a speaking engagement at corporations, my agent and I now reckon we can tell within three phone calls whether a company is running on confidence or on fear — and if it's the latter, I almost always find a polite excuse and walk away.' His holistic approach to his job and his philosophizing has earnt him a bad name in the British press, who like their heroes to conform to type. What the Press fail to see is that Cleese, for all his common sense and guru-worship, is a true British character.

One occasionally detects a feeling in the Press of being let down because John Cleese, one of the funniest men on the planet, has spent a lot of time not being funny any more. The fact is, comedy is no longer Cleese's sole interest. At heart he is a serious sort of person and this seriousness is frequently mistaken for solemnity. Unlike nearly almost every other comic born, Cleese has almost no ambition to be funny when he's not being paid to be so. When he gives interviews, he comes across as good humoured rather than side-splittingly funny, though for the Americans, he works harder on the gags and seems to play up the culture gap. He recently itemized three differences between the English and the Americans for one US TV programme as follows: 1) we speak English and you don't; 2) when we hold a world championship for a particular sport, we invite teams from other countries; 3) when we meet a head of state in England, we only go down on one knee.

FURRY THINGS

Perhaps the most engaging feature of John Cleese's career in the last years of the 1990s came as a result of the affair that Cleese had with an inmate at Bristol Zoo. If you look at *Monty Python's* obsession with ferrets, pantomime horses and animals of various sorts, the move will come as no surprise. Working with different creatures and dabbling in green issues was to come to a head in one of the unquestionable masterpieces of Cleese's recent career — a remarkable BBC wildlife programme on his first love: lemurs. It was called *Born To Be Wild: Operation Lemur* and was

Right: With chum Michael Winner, whose Death Wish *films were the inspiration for* Fierce Creatures' *early working title –* Death Fish 2.
Overleaf: Tell young folk that today and they won't believe you – the 'Four Yorkshiremen' sketch, with Roman Atkinson, in The Secret Policeman's Ball.

broadcast in the summer of 1998.

Here was the man who had sanctioned fish torture in *A Fish Called Wanda* and threatened to exterminate half a zoo in *Fierce Creatures*. Now he was cuddling the critters like long-lost friends. In truth, Cleese has always been mad about animals. As a boy, he kept a cat, but the ring-tailed lemur he met at Bristol Zoo set off something altogether different in the young Cleese. For five years after they first met, he brought it bananas.

'I think the English have some great qualities, but we are not the most physically comfortable of nations,' he explained to Max Davidson in an interview for the *Daily Telegraph* to plug the programme. Davidson couldn't help noticing that the Cleese household was stuffed with animals — a fluffy octopus, a stuffed panda and assorted Womble-like viscose fauna.

'For English children of my generation, touching people was out because it had sexual connotations,' Cleese explained to Davidson. 'But nobody would bat an eyelid if you stroked a cat. I think touch is far more important than people realise. Why do you think Margaret Thatcher attached such importance to her visits to the hairdresser? Because she knew she could be groomed and touched for an hour without anyone minding.'

John got to meet his old flame when he put £50,000 into a conservation project based at Jersey Zoo (his favourite place on earth) to reintroduce some members of this engaging species to its native Madagascar, where populations of these strange beasts are sadly dwindling. The upshot was a delightful programme, with Cleese on terrific form, talking in Johnny Morris fashion to the animals and sending up the whole wildlife genre at the same time. The highlight is a three-second shot of Cleese swinging across a clearing in the jungle, mimicking the lemur's upright sideways walk. He was dressed in a tail coat to prove his point that the lemur's gait resembles an Edwardian wine waiter on Benzedrine.

It was a cheering to see Cleese doing a show in which he was funny and interesting. He also got in a gentle dig at Michael Palin, whose genial trips around the world have turned him into the country's top travel documentarist.

COASTING AGAIN

Every time an anniversary year comes around, John is asked the same question: 'Will the boys ever get together again?' The Pythons haven't performed live for nearly twenty years. John says he spends more time answering questions about the series than he ever did in making it. He got so fed up with the 'when-will-you-reform?' question that he told one Italian journalist that a reunion was impossible. The man asked why. 'Because they're all dead apart from me. Except for Terry Jones, and he's suffering from a terminal illness and has lost control of all his bodily functions. So if you go to see him, wear protective clothing.'

All the same, the team — including Graham Chapman's ashes in an urn — got together in Aspen, Colorado, in March 1998 for the US Comedy Arts Festival. They presented a *Python* retrospective on the final night, which was then cut into a one-hour TV special, of which John rather approved. This was the first time they had been seen together on stage since *The Secret Policeman's Ball* in 1979. In fact, it all went so swimmingly that they then announced that they were considering a ten-week stage tour for the following year — 1999 — their thirtieth anniversary. But it has yet to happen. Part of the problem is that none of them are keen to do just the old stuff, which is what the fans want. They want to do new sketches as well, which means writing the material.

The writing process ground to a halt years ago. The team now get on well — though only in short bursts — but without Chapman around, the old writing formula is unbalanced. Still, there was enough nostalgia in the air after the retrospective for all of them to entertain the idea. On an American chat show after the event, John pointed out something he hadn't thought of: it was to do with fun.

'Terry Jones at Aspen said something that struck me as quite perceptive. He said the greatest moment was writing the sketch and reading it out to each other. But then we had to go and put the bloody thing on television. The moment of utter pleasure was making them [the others] fall around.' Everything afterwards — the filming — was an anti-climax. Tedium was the price the Pythons paid for getting the work on screen. And it was boredom that caused John to leave the group. It may also be the reason why the tour has been put on hold: getting anything to work on stage is twice as demanding as cooking up a sketch for the screen.

When a TV station in Chicago recently screened a *Monty Python* marathon (forty-two episodes shown consecutively), John did a promo for the event and happily went back into patter: 'We're hoping you're finding this twenty-two-hour marathon educational,' he announced. 'You're learning about Spam, the Spanish Inquisition, how to recognise different types of trees from quite a long way away and other basic life lessons. So stay tuned and don't quit watching until your brain starts to hurt.'

Cleese can still do the old banter, but writing anything fresh — well, that's a different story. As he explained on American TV — he does a lot of American TV, as audiences are familiar with his face following his celebrated guest appearance on *Cheers* as the psychologist Simon Finch-Royce — he is still deeply irked by requests for funny voices and silly walks. His American host asked him what he did with people who pester him for 'The Parrot' sketch: 'I get them beaten up by my bodyguards,' said John. 'They're very nice guys, the bodyguards, and they do it with great taste, but they do beat the shit out of them.' The deadpan delivery must have left a few of the American audience wondering exactly who this British gangster-actor was.

In fact John has never really been keen on resurrections. The sequel to *A Fish Called Wanda* must have taught him that the past is best left alone. Still, fans live in hope. There's plenty to amuse them: it's extraordinary how global the appeal of the *Python* team still remains. The Internet is groaning with geeky compilations of trivia and lists of Cleese's appearances, advertisements and projects. There's even a CD-Rom full of *Python* computer gizmos in the making.

Meanwhile, John has carried on working on films including *Parting Shots*, directed by Michael Winner (an unlikely friend of the Cleeses), and *The Out-Of-Towners* (the original 1970 film was a none-too-hot Jack Lemmon film with a script by Neil Simon) in which he played a hotel concierge — shades of Fawlty revisited, perhaps? — to good reviews in America.

Muriel, John's mother, is still alive and well and, at the time of writing, she is approaching 100 years of age. John keeps in close touch with her. Alyce Faye, his third wife, has recently published a book called *How To Manage Your Mother*. She interviewed dozens of women about their mothers and slapped a Cleesian title on the cover. The book is rather touching. She told Suzie MacKenzie in the *Evening*

With Alyce Faye and assorted fauna at the Fierce Creatures *film premiere in Los Angeles.*

Standard that 'if you asked John, he would say that his relationship with his mother has been very intense but now it is quite good.' After 60 years, so it should be. Lately, Muriel complained that she had had enough and wished to die. John, instead of consoling his beloved mum as one might expect, replied, 'Fine. I'll arrange for someone to come round to kill you then.'

Lurking beneath the dire cardigans and reasonableness, the tallest comedian of his generation is still capable of the unexpected. A scare with prostate cancer turned out to be phoney, but it still drew him up short. The ensuing 'my-battle-with-cancer' interviews were, for a while, a very real and frightening prospect. But as Cleese drifts into the future — still unfeatured by *Hello!* magazine — the fact is that, whatever happens, his fans have already stuffed and mounted him in the most hallowed end of the hall of comedy heroes. **John Cleese**

PICTURE CREDITS

Alpha p82,85,90,97,98,111,121,127. Alpha/Tim Anderson
p6,13 Alpha/Richard Chambury p48. Alpha/Dave Parker p121
Camera Press/T Leighton p10. Camera Press/Richard Open p104.
Camera Press/John Wildgoose p103
The Kobal Collection p18,37,60,69,72,86,107,108,122,123. The Kobal
Collection/David Appleby p116. The Kobal Collection/Frank Conner p115
Moviestore Collection p14. Moviestore Collection/BBC p9,43
Pictorial Press p20,23,25,26,33,35,38,44,47,51,54,57,58,
63,66,67,70,75,78,81,93,94,108,118

BIBLIOGRAPHY

Jonathan Margolis, *Cleese Encounters* (Orion)
David Nathan, *The Laughtermakers* (Peter Owen)
Graham Chapman, *A Liar's Autobiography* (Methuen)
Robert Ross, *Monty Python Encyclopedia* (Batsford)
Morwenna Banks and Amanda Swift, *The Joke's On Us* (Pandora)
Robert Hewison, *Footlights* (Methuen)
George Perry, *A Life Of Python* (Pavilion Books)
Roger Wilmut, *From Fringe to Flying Circus* (Eyre Methuen)
John Cleese and Robin Skynner, *Families & How To Survive Them* (Hutchinson)

SOURCES

Magazines: *Tatler, Options, Harpers & Queen, Sight And Sound, Plays & Players*
Newspapers: *Daily Telegraph, Sunday Telegraph, The Times, The Sunday Times,
Independent, Guardian, Observer, Daily Mail, Mail On Sunday, Express,
Sunday Express, Mirror*

DISCLAIMER